VGM Opportunities Series

# OPPORTUNITIES IN ENTERTAINMENT CAREERS

## Jan Goldberg

Foreword by
**Lillie Yvette Salinas**
Actress

**VGM Career Horizons**
*NTC/Contemporary Publishing Group*

**Library of Congress Cataloging-in-Publication Data**

Goldberg, Jan.
    Opportunities in entertainment careers / Jan Goldberg.
        p.  cm. — (VGM opportunities series)
    ISBN 0-8442-1819-7 (cloth). — ISBN 0-8442-1829-4 (pbk.)
    1. Performing arts—Vocational guidance.   2. Music—Vocational
guidance. I. Title.   II. Series.
PN1580.G5688   1999
791'.023—dc21                                          98-46030
                                                           CIP

**Cover Photo Credits:**
Top right, copyright © 1997 Susan Aurinko Photography, Chicago; top left, bottom left and right, images copyright © 1997 PhotoDisc, Inc.

Published by VGM Career Horizons
A division of NTC/Contemporary Publishing Group, Inc.
4255 West Touhy Avenue, Lincolnwood (Chicago), Illinois 60646-1975 U.S.A.
Copyright © 1999 by NTC/Contemporary Publishing Group, Inc.
Printed in the United States of America
International Standard Book Number:  0-8442-1819-7 (cloth)
                                                          0-8442-1829-4 (paper)

99  00  01  02  03  04  MV  18  17  16  15  14  13  12  11  10 9  8  7  6  5  4  3  2  1

# DEDICATION

This book is dedicated to a special uncle, Bernard Lefko.

# CONTENTS

**About the Author** . . . . . . . . . . . . . . . . . . . . . . . . . . . . . . . . . . . . . . . . . **vii**

**Foreword** . . . . . . . . . . . . . . . . . . . . . . . . . . . . . . . . . . . . . . . . . . . . . . . . .**ix**

**Acknowledgments** . . . . . . . . . . . . . . . . . . . . . . . . . . . . . . . . . . . . . . . . . .**xi**

**1. Careers in Acting** . . . . . . . . . . . . . . . . . . . . . . . . . . . . . . . . . . . . . . . **1**

The world of acting. Training and qualifications. Strategies for finding a job. Job outlook. Salaries. Profiles. For more information.

**2. Careers in Music and Dance** . . . . . . . . . . . . . . . . . . . . . . . . . . . . **24**

Musicians. Dancers. Training for musicians. Training for dancers. Job outlook for musicians. Job outlook for dancers. Salaries for musicians. Salaries for dancers. Profiles. For more information.

**3. Careers in Radio and Television** . . . . . . . . . . . . . . . . . . . . . . . . **52**

The world of radio and television. On the job. Training and qualifications. Building a career. Job outlook. Salaries. Profiles. For more information.

**4. Careers Behind the Scenes** . . . . . . . . . . . . . . . . . . . . . . . . . . . . . **68**

Jobs behind the scenes in music. Jobs behind the scenes in acting. Training for careers behind the scenes in music. Training for careers behind the scenes in acting. Job outlook for careers behind the scenes in music. Job outlook for careers behind the scenes in acting. Salaries for careers behind the scenes in music. Salaries for careers behind the scenes in acting. Profiles. For more information.

5. **The Business of Entertainment** . . . . . . . . . . . . . . . . . . . . . . . . . .**95**

Artists' representatives or personal/business managers. Producers. Casting directors. General managers. Company managers. Box office managers. House managers. Touring production managers. Theatrical press agents. Training for the business of entertainment in music. Training for the business of entertainment in acting. Job outlook for the business of entertainment in music. Job outlook for the business of entertainment in acting. Salaries for the business of entertainment in music. Salaries for the business of entertainment in acting. Profiles. For more information.

6. **Teaching Music and Acting** . . . . . . . . . . . . . . . . . . . . . . . . . . . . . .**113**

Teaching music. Teaching theater. Training for music teachers. Training for theater teachers. Salaries for music teachers. Salaries for theater teachers. Career outlook for music teachers. Career outlook for theater teachers. Job strategies. Profiles. For more information.

7. **Careers in Writing** . . . . . . . . . . . . . . . . . . . . . . . . . . . . . . . . . . . . .**133**

Composer. Songwriter. Arranger. Playwright. Screenwriter. Drama (or theater) critic. On the job. Training for composers, songwriters, and arrangers. Training for playwrights, screenwriters, and critics. Salaries for composers, songwriters, and arrangers. Salaries for playwrights, screenwriters, and critics. Career outlook. Profiles. For more information.

# ABOUT THE AUTHOR

Jan Goldberg's love for the printed page began well before her second birthday. Regular visits to the book bindery where her grandfather worked produced a magic combination of sights and smells that she carries with her to this day.

Childhood was filled with composing poems and stories, reading books, and playing library. Elementary and high school included an assortment of contributions to school newspapers. While a full-time college student, Goldberg wrote extensively as part of her job responsibilities in the College of Business Administration at Roosevelt University in Chicago. After receiving a degree in elementary education, she was able to extend her love of reading and writing to her students.

Goldberg has written extensively in the occupations area for General Learning Corporation's *Career World Magazine,* as well as for the many career publications produced by CASS Communications. The four children's career books she authored for Capstone Publishing Company will be published before the end of the year. She also has contributed to a number of projects for educational publishers, including Scott Foresman, Addison-Wesley, and Camp Fire Boys and Girls.

As a feature writer, Goldberg's work has appeared in *Parenting Magazine, Today's Chicago Woman, Opportunity Magazine, Chicago Parent, Correspondent, Opportunity Magazine, Successful Student, Family Software Magazine, Complete Woman, North Shore Magazine,* and the Pioneer Press newspapers. In all, she has published more than three hundred pieces as a full-time freelance writer.

In addition to *Opportunities in Entertainment Careers,* she is the author of more than a dozen other career books published by NTC/Contemporary Publishing Group, Inc.

# FOREWORD

My journey as a performer began at the age of four. My parents saw to it that I was enrolled in ballet class. What started out as a weekly dance class to ensure that I didn't turn into a tomboy (having four older brothers) eventually led to daily classes in ballet, jazz, pointe, modern, flamenco, folklorico, and tap by the age of ten. From my first love—dance—I learned discipline, perseverance, and to express myself without words.

Having undergone a total knee reconstruction in my early twenties, my days as a dancer came to an end. From this "tragedy" I found my second love and true passion—acting. As performers, we all have our "turning points," the moment at which we realize that what we want from life could only come from performing. The role that changed my life was my most challenging and demanding, yet, touching role—Helen Keller in *The Miracle Worker*. It was through my portrayal of Helen that I realized that through acting you can reach others, touch them, and make them feel a range of emotions. It was then that my dream of becoming a professional actress was born.

While for many the ultimate goal is to break into show business, being a performer is a difficult job. There is no such thing as a typical, nine-to-five workday. There are endless hours of auditions, rehearsals, shows, photo sessions, phone calls, and dozens of other tasks to attend to. Also inherent in the job is the waiting for phone calls, the rejection notices, and the voice and acting lessons! This is not to mention juggling the part-time jobs you need to pay the bills and survive. However, while it may not be easy, there is no greater feeling than when you are up on stage and you have the audience right in the palm of your hand. This is what acting is about—love and passion for the art of performing.

In my professional career I have modeled, performed in various theater productions, done radio commercials, been photographed in print ads, and appeared as an extra in a made-for-television movie and feature-length film. All of these opportunities have provided me with wonderful experiences, great memories, and substantial acting credentials. However, it is my acting for schoolchildren that I find most gratifying and meaningful. I look upon these performances as nontraditional teaching. By bringing children and the art of performing together, I am able to teach and encourage children's interest in theater, dance, and music. I not only cultivate their interest in the arts, but assist with teaching them self-expression, imagination, creativity, a better understanding of the world they live in, and, most of all, appreciation for the performing arts.

While I may not be a household name, if I have touched the life of one child through my acting, then I know I have accomplished something important. I offer these words of advice, "Hold fast to your dreams, follow your inner voice, and be willing to share your gift of performing. It will be through your self-expression, dedication, and passion to your art that you will be able to touch and influence the lives of others. And by doing so, you will have made a difference."

Lillie Yvette Salinas
Actress
Greater Kansas City area

# ACKNOWLEDGMENTS

The author gratefully acknowledges:

- The numerous professionals who graciously agreed to be profiled in this book.
- My dear husband, Larry, for his inspiration and vision.
- My children, Deborah, Bruce, and Sherri, for their encouragement and love.
- Family and close friends—Adrienne, Marty, Mindi, Cary, Michele, Paul, Michele, Alison, Steve, Marci, Steven, Brian, Jesse, Bertha, Uncle Bernard, and Aunt Helen for their faith and support.
- Diana Catlin, for her insights and input.
- Betsy Lancefield, editor at VGM, for making all projects rewarding and enjoyable.

# CHAPTER 1

# CAREERS IN ACTING

I have to act to live.
—Laurence Olivier

Have you always been able to "act" your way out of situations (pleasant or otherwise)? Have you been routinely able to convince people that your intentions are genuine (whether they were or not)? Have you always sought out an audience and longed for attention and applause for your performing talents? Perhaps, the world of acting is beckoning to you!

What's it like to be an actor? Is it all glamour and fun? How does one plan a career in acting? How difficult is it to achieve success as an actor? All of these important questions will be answered in this chapter.

## THE WORLD OF ACTING

Based on scripts, actors perform their roles in theaters, movies, and radio and television productions. Whether the characters they are portraying are young or old, or the part is dramatic or comedic, actors bring their characters "to life" using voices, gestures, and movements.

Though acting is often viewed as a glamorous profession, the truth is that many actors are forced to put in long and irregular hours (including rehearsals and performances) with little payment in return. In addition only a few actors achieve recognition as stars on the stage, in motion pictures, or on television. A somewhat larger number are well-known, experienced performers who frequently are cast in supporting roles. Most actors struggle to break into the profession and pick up parts wherever they can. Many successful actors continue to accept small roles, including commercials and product endorsements. Some actors employed by theater companies teach acting courses to the public.

### On the Job

Acting demands patience and total commitment, because there are often long periods of unemployment between jobs and rejections when auditioning for work. And while under contract, actors are frequently required to work long hours and travel. Evening work is a regular part of a stage actor's life.

In order to secure a part, actors must audition. If they are selected for a role, they must memorize their lines and rehearse with other cast members—often for approximately three to four weeks. It's important for each actor to understand his or her character and for each personality to mesh with the others in the production. Flawless performances require tedious memorizing of lines and repetitive rehearsals.

## TRAINING AND QUALIFICATIONS

Successful actors recommend that those who aspire to this profession should take part in high school and college plays for the experience these activities provide. Large cities like Chicago, New York, and Los Angeles have public high schools especially for the performing arts.

Formal dramatic training and/or acting experience is generally necessary, although some people enter the field without either. Training can be obtained at dramatic arts schools in New York and Los Angeles and at colleges and universities throughout the country offering bachelor's or higher degrees in dramatic and theater arts. A master's degree in theater is considered an additional plus. Most people take college courses in liberal arts, theater, directing, play production, design, playwriting, speech and movement, practical courses in acting, and dramatic literature. Many experienced actors get additional formal training to learn new skills and improve on old ones.

### Desirable Qualities

Desirable personal qualities for actors include talent, determination, perseverance, persistence, social skills, a good memory, a fine speaking voice, creative ability, and training that will enable them to portray different characters. Training in singing and dancing is especially useful. Actors must have poise, stage presence, the ability to affect an audience, plus the ability to follow directions. Physical appearance is often a deciding factor in being selected for particular roles.

Actors need stamina to withstand the heat of stage or studio lights, heavy costumes, the long and irregular hours, and the adverse weather conditions that may exist on location.

## Building a Career

The best way to start building an acting career is to pursue local opportunities and then move on from there. Acting groups and local and regional theater experience may help in obtaining work in New York or Los Angeles. Modeling experience also may be helpful.

Most actors list themselves with casting agencies that help them find parts. Many also take advantage of the services offered by the unions listed at the end of this chapter. Many professional actors rely on agents or managers to find work, negotiate contracts, and plan their careers. Agents generally earn a percentage of an actor's contract.

As actors' reputations grow, they work on larger productions or in more prestigious theaters. Actors also advance to lead or specialized roles. A few actors move into acting-related jobs as drama coaches or directors of stage, television, radio, or motion picture productions. Some teach drama in colleges and universities.

The length of a performer's working life depends largely on training, skill, versatility, and perseverance. Some actors continue working throughout their lives; however, many leave the occupation after a short time because they cannot find enough work to make a living.

## Extra—Extra—Read All About It!

In addition to the actors with speaking parts, extras, who have small parts with no lines to deliver, are used throughout the industry. To become a movie extra (also known as a background artist), one must usually be listed by a casting agency such as Central Casting, a no-fee agency that supplies all extras to the major movie studios in Hollywood. Applicants are accepted only when the number of persons of a particular type on the list is below the foreseeable need. In recent years, only a very small proportion of the applicants have succeeded in being listed.

## STRATEGIES FOR FINDING A JOB

Armed with your college degree, basic knowledge of the acting business, and some experience, you'll need to prepare a portfolio that will highlight your qualifications, acting history, and special skills. This will take the form of a resume. You also will need to have photos taken by a professional photographer (one who shows you off to your best advantage). These are the essential tools of your trade. Attach your resume to the back of your picture with one staple at the upper left and right hand corners. Once you have your portfolio ready, you can start making the rounds of casting offices, ad agencies, producers' offices, and agents. Several trade newspapers contain casting information, ads for part-time jobs, information about shows, and other pertinent data about what's going on in the industry. Among these are *Back Stage* in New York and Los Angeles and *Ross Reports* in New York. There is also the weekly *Variety.* In Los Angeles there's also *Daily Variety,* the *Hollywood Reporter,* and *Drama-Logue.* You will even be able to find out about casting calls and other opportunities on-line through the Internet.

Once your drop off your resumes and head shots, you certainly shouldn't just sit at home waiting for the phone to ring. It's wise to stay in contact, so stop by and say hello. Check in by phone every week to see if any opportunities are available for you. If you are currently in a show, send prospective employers a flyer. It shows them that you are a working actor.

When you get past this initial stage and actually win an audition, here are some things you should remember:

*Audition Tips*

1. Be prepared.
2. Be familiar with the piece; read it beforehand and choose the parts you'd like to try out for.
3. Go for it—don't hold back.
4. Speak loudly and clearly and project to the back of the room.
5. Take chances.

6. Try not to be the first one to audition. If you can, observe others so that you can pick up on what the evaluators seem to like or dislike.
7. Appear enthusiastic and confident.
8. Keep auditioning even if you don't get parts. You are getting invaluable experience that is bound to pay off.

So—when do you get an agent? Not just yet.

First of all, you don't need an agent to audition for everything. There are many things you can audition for that do not require an agent, such as theater, nonunion films, and union films. However, most commercials are cast through agencies, so you would most likely need an agent to land one of those.

While waiting to be chosen for a part, acting hopefuls often take jobs as waitresses, bartenders, taxi drivers, etc. These jobs provide a more flexible schedule and some money to live on.

## JOB OUTLOOK

Employment of actors is expected to grow faster than the average for all occupations through the year 2005. Rising foreign demand for American productions, combined with a growing domestic market fueled by the growth of cable television, home movie rentals, and television syndications, should stimulate demand for actors and other production personnel.

The growth of opportunities in recorded media should be accompanied by increasing jobs in live productions. More and more people who enjoy live theatrical entertainment will continue to go to theaters for excitement and aesthetics.

Touring productions of Broadway plays and other large shows are offering new opportunities for actors. However, employment may be somewhat affected by government funding for the arts. A decline in funding could dampen future employment growth in this segment of the entertainment industry.

Even with all of the positives mentioned, it is important to know that acting is still considered an overcrowded field and is expected to remain so for the foreseeable future. This is because the large number of people desiring acting careers and the lack of formal entry requirements will continue to cause keen competition for acting jobs. Only the most talented will find regular employment. There will always be a greater number of actors than there are roles for them to play.

## SALARIES

Minimum salaries, hours of work, and other conditions of employment are covered in collective bargaining agreements between producers of shows and unions representing workers in this field. The Actors' Equity Association represents stage actors; the Screen Actors Guild (SAG) and the Screen Extras Guild cover actors in motion pictures, including television, commercials, and films; and the American Federation of Television and Radio Artists (AFTRA) represents television and radio performers. Of course, any actor may negotiate for a salary higher than the minimum.

According to limited information, the minimum weekly salary for actors in Broadway stage productions is $1,000. Those in small off-Broadway theaters receive minimums ranging from $380 to $650 a week, depending on the seating capacity of the theater. For shows on the road, actors receive about $100 per day more for living expenses.

Actors usually work long hours during rehearsals. Once the show opens, they have more regular hours and work about thirty hours per week.

According to the Screen Actors Guild, motion picture and television actors with speaking parts earn a minimum daily rate of about $500, or $1,750 for a five-day week. Those without speaking parts, the extras, earn a minimum daily rate of about $100. Actors also receive contributions to their health and pension plans and additional compensation for reruns.

Earnings from acting are low because employment is so irregular. The Screen Actors Guild also reports that the average income its members earn from acting is $1,400 a year, and 80 percent of its members earn less than $5,000 a year from acting. Therefore, many actors must supplement their incomes by holding jobs in other fields.

Some well-known actors have salary rates well above the minimums, and the salaries of the few top stars are many times the figures cited, creating a false impression that all actors are highly paid. Many actors who work more than a set number of weeks per year are covered by a union health, welfare, and pension fund, including hospitalization insurance, to which employers contribute. Under some employment conditions, Actors' Equity and AFTRA members have paid vacations and sick leave.

## PROFILES

### Meet Jennifer Aquino

Jennifer Aquino studied theater and dance at the University of California in Los Angeles and received a Bachelor of Arts degree in economics. As a member of the dance team, she was a UCLA cheerleader for three years. In addition to cheering for UCLA's football and basketball teams, she also entered national dance team competitions.

"I grew up in Cerritos, California, and received my first taste of acting at St. Linus elementary school in Norwalk, where I played the leading role of the princess in *Beyond the Horizon,* says Aquino. "Happily, I received the Performing Arts Award while attending Whitney High School.

"Following my college graduation, I got my first break playing Eolani, the wife of Dr. Jacoby in David Lynch's television series *Twin Peaks.* (The result of my very first audition!). Then I got an agent and joined the Screen Actors Guild. I have been performing in various theatrical productions and am a founding member of Theatre Geo, as well as an active member of Theatre West and the East West Players Network. (Watch for me in a national commercial for Ford trucks.)

"My television credits include: *Weird Science; The Paranormal Borderline, Fresh Prince of Bel Air, Santa Barbara,* and *Twin Peaks.*

"Film credits include: *The Party Crashers, Prisoners of Love,* AFI's *it makes you wonder…how a girl can keep from going under,* UCLA's *Fleeting Vanities of Life,* USC's *Unexpected Love,* and NYU's *Free Love.*

"Theater credits include: *People Like Me* at the Playwrights Arena; *Gila River* at Japan America Theatre and at Scottsdale Center for the Arts in Arizona; *Cabaret* and *Sophisticated Barflies* at East West Players; the PAWS/LA Gala Benefit at the Pasadena Playhouse; the S.T.A.G.E. Benefit at the Luckman Theatre; *The Really Early Dinner Theatre for Kids* at The Hollywood Playhouse; *Boys' Life, Hold Me!, Scruples,* and *Watermelon Boats* at Theatre West; *Mistletoe Mews* at Theatre Geo; and *Is Nudity Required?* at Playhouse of the Foothills.

"I remember performing at family gatherings ever since I was a small child," says Aquino. "I always enjoyed being in the spotlight. To me, acting is like a child's game of pretend, something I always enjoyed. I see it as a career where you can earn a lot of money, while having a lot of fun. At the same time, you are entertaining people, impacting them, making them think, helping them to feel certain emotions, educating them, and helping them escape from their current lives.

"Most actors who are starting out hold some kind of side job, day job, or part-time job. For me it was a career in the health care industry working for Kaiser Foundation Health Plan. I then became a health care consultant for one of the big six accounting firms, Deloitte & Touche LLP. I was such a good employee that my managers would be flexible and let me go out on auditions.

"After a few years I realized that I was working too many hours, seventy to eighty per week, and I finally had to make a decision to quit my day job and focus 100 percent of my time toward acting. After booking a few jobs, including a national commercial, I was able to do so. It was a big risk, but one I felt necessary to take. I remember what my acting coach would say, 'part-time work gets part-time results.' The more I put into acting, the more I got out of it.

"Don't be fooled," stresses Aquino. "Acting is a lot of hard work! I am at it seven days a week, mornings, afternoons, evenings, weekends—forty to sixty hours per week. And if I'm not working on the creative side of acting, which is doing my homework for a job that I booked or for an audition, I am working on the business side of acting—talking to my agents and managers; networking; sending my head shots to casting directors, producers, and writers; attending seminars; meeting people; etc. I also try to keep my stress level down and take care of myself by getting enough sleep and exercise, eating healthy, and having some relaxation time. And I have been fortunate; the sets I've worked on have all been positive experiences for me.

"What I like most about my work is that I can say that I am making a living doing what I absolutely love to do, and that I am pursuing my passion in life. Not too many people in this world can say that. What I like least about my work is that there are a lot of politics in it. It's not always the best actor who gets the job. Some of the time it's a certain look, what your credits are, who you know, etc., that determines who gets the job. There are a lot of things that are out of your control. That's just part of the business and you have to accept it.

"I would advise anyone who is considering acting as a career to pursue your dreams and be persistent—but only if it's something you absolutely love to do, and there's nothing else in the world you would rather do. Pursue the creative as well as the business side of acting. Don't let anyone stop you from doing what you want to do. And always keep up your craft by continuing your training."

## Meet Gonzo Schexnayder

Gonzo Schexnayder earned a bachelor's degree in journalism and advertising at Louisiana State University in Baton Rouge. He attended various acting classes at LSU and Monterey Peninsula College in Monterey, California. He also attended Chicago's Second City Training Center for more than a year and The Actors Center following that. He is a SAG and AFTRA member.

"I had always wanted to do stand-up comedy but didn't pursue it until graduating from college when I began working with an improvisational comedy group," explains Schexnayder. "Four months later, the military sent me to Monterey, California, for language training. While there, I did my first staged reading and my first show. I'd never felt such elation as when I performed. Nothing in my life had given me the sheer thrill and rush that I experienced by creating a character and maintaining that throughout a given period of time. Nothing else mattered but that moment on stage, my other actors, and the scene we were performing.

"After completing the language program in November of 1990, I returned to Baton Rouge. There I began the long process of introspection about my career choices and what I wanted to do. I began to audition locally and started reading and studying acting. I still had not made the jump to being an actor; I was merely investigating the possibility.

"One night while watching an interview with John Goodman, I realized how important acting had become to me. I knew that it possibly meant a life of macaroni and cheese and noodles, but I knew that up until that moment, nothing had made me as happy or as motivated. While I believed I had the skills and the drive to make it in advertising or whatever career I chose, I decided that acting was my only logical choice.

"Whether it's rehearsing a show, performing improvisation in front of an audience, or even auditioning for a commercial, it's fun. If you can separate the sense of rejection most actors feel from not getting a part, auditioning for anything becomes your job. Rehearsing becomes your life. Just as a carpenter's job is building a house, as an actor, I look at my job as building my performance. The final product is there for me to look at and admire (if executed well), but the path to that product is the thrill.

"Unfortunately, I'm not at a point in my career where I'm making enough money to quit my day job. I'm close, but not close enough. I still feel the need to have some sense of financial stability or I lapse into thinking about money. It's all about balance and deciding what's really important. Sure I'd love to have an apartment with central air and a balcony. I'd love to have a car that is still under warranty. But, I know that by putting my efforts and money into my acting career, those other things don't matter. What matters is how it makes me feel. Cars and apartments don't give me the satisfaction that being an actor does.

"How many hours I work and how busy I am depends on what I'm doing. Over the last year I've worked with five other actors to open our own theater—Broad Shoulders Theatre—and have found my time constrained. On top of that I have been pursuing, with some success, a voice-over/on-camera career in addition to working a full-time job. Yesterday I finished six days of shooting on a graduate thesis film, and last weekend we opened our first show (TheatreSports/Chicago, Improvisational Comedy) at our new theater. We have another opening—which I'm not performing in—tonight and expect to open four more shows in the next three months. I've also taken a year of guitar classes and maintained my presence in acting/on-camera classes and workshops. I'm always busy and continually looking for the next chance to market myself and increase my salability as an actor (train, study, perform, work).

"I love the process of acting and sometimes just the fast-paced, eclectic nature of the business. There is always something new to learn and something new to try. The sheer excitement of performing live is amazing, and the personal satisfaction of getting an audience to laugh or cry simply by your words and actions is very gratifying.

"There are many people who take advantage of an actor's desire to perform. As one of the only professions where there is an abundance of people willing to work for nothing, producers/casting directors/agents/managers who only care about the money will take advantage of and abuse actors for personal gain. Being an astute actor helps prevent much of this, but one must always be on the lookout.

"I would advise others who are interested in this career to work where you are. Perfect your craft. Move when you 'have' to—you will know when it's time. And above all, trust your instincts."

## Meet Jack Stauffer

Jack Stauffer, a graduate of Northwestern University, has been a working actor since 1968. He created the role of Chuck Tyler in the popular television daytime drama, *All My Children,* and remained in that role for three and a half years (386 shows). Other regular television appearances include *Battlestar Galactica* and *Young and Restless.* Episodic television appearances include *Lois and Clark, Viper, Designing Women, Quantum Leap, Perfect Strangers, Growing Pains, Knotts Landing,* and *Dynasty.* In all, he has appeared in forty prime-time television shows and numerous movies-of-the-week and miniseries. He was also co-star in the movie, *Chattanooga Choo Choo.* In theater, he had parts in *My Fair Lady* and *Oliver* at the Grove Theatre in San Bernadino County. Other play productions include *The Music Man, Annie Get Your Gun, Fiorello, Can Can, The Music Man, Mister Roberts,* and *Guys and Dolls.* His list of achievements also includes parts in more than two hundred commercials.

"I started as a child actor, but really didn't become a professional until I graduated from college in 1968," says Stauffer. "I simply sold my car, moved to New York, and hit the pavement!

"I grew up in the industry. My mother worked for Warner Brothers and was W. C. Fields's radio producer. My father produced the *March of Time* for radio during WWII. He then founded his own advertising agency and was responsible for many early television series in the days when the ad agencies had tremendous creative input into a television show. Many notable celebrities used to spend time in our living room. As long as I can remember, I have always wanted to be a performer. It has been my burning desire despite my parents' best efforts to dissuade me from the vagaries of the industry. They would have been happy for me to pursue a more stable and lucrative career.

"Unless you are on a series or are a celebrity, you are constantly battling the belief that you will probably never work again. Thus, your workday consists of looking everywhere and calling any one who might give you a job. Once you have done all you can do, you inevitably wait for the phone to ring. The vast majority of the time, it doesn't. So, most actors have other jobs—temporary work, or selling, or in my case, teaching tennis—anything to make enough money to pay the bills so you can pursue your craft. When you are finally hired for a day or a week or a month or whatever it might be, every moment in your day suddenly has purpose. You get to do what you were meant to do, even if it is only for a short time or if the part is minuscule. You are on top of the world. Then it is over, and it is back to square one.

"The best thing about your work is the work itself. An actor lives by his emotions and his ability to convey them to an audience. A good actor makes it look easy even though it is very hard. That is why so many actors work for free. It is the work that fulfills them. Of course, if you get paid, it is much better. The recognition factor is important also. That is why so many actors return to the stage. The gratification is immediate. Any actor who says the applause means nothing to him is probably lying.

"The worst thing about the industry is that absolute lack of tenure. You are only as good as your next job. Your history, experience, etc., don't mean much. This is because there is no studio system any more. With no continuity, it is difficult to slowly work your way up the ladder of success. The easiest way to get hired today is to have the executive producer of a hit show as your brother-in-law.

"The question I am asked more than any other is how to get into this industry, and the answer is easy. If you have an absolute, undying, uncontrollable passion to do this—and I mean you will die if you don't—then by all means give it everything you have got. But, if you are the slightest bit timid or unsure, choose another career. This is a business based on rejection, and it can destroy you. If you sell cars and somebody doesn't buy one, they simply don't want that car. As an actor, when you are turned down, they don't want *you*. It's difficult *not* to take it personally. You have to be very strong to keep at it."

### Meet Joseph Bowman

Joseph Bowman is an actor in the Los Angeles area. He is a high school graduate who has some college, vocational, and military training. He also participated in the Vanguard Theatre Ensemble Training for four years. He considers himself at the beginning of his acting career.

"I was in the Marine Corps for six years and attained the rank of Sergeant via Meritorious Promotion," says Bowman. " I thoroughly loved the United States Military Corp. It tended to reward a person who acted as if he enjoyed this kind of life, and I was such a person. It seems that I have always been able to act appropriately in any given situation. Older people usually find me charming. Younger people usually find me cool. I love to be the chameleon.

"Five years ago, a friend was attending a model/talent showcase that piqued my interest. I ended up doing it, and he didn't. Even though it was a fiasco, it had revived in me my love of performing.

"At my present level, I do a lot of background work. My military experience gets me a lot of work in productions that have a need for people who have 'been there' to add a flavor that normal actors don't always possess. Much of this work involves firing military weapons (blanks) and the knowledge of the safety concerns therein.

"There are not many typical days in acting because every production is very different. It is like working for a different company in a different capacity every day. I may be asked to simply put on a costume and chat (mime) with another actor for eight hours one day. Another day I might be asked to put on the full battle dress uniform of a branch of the military and fire an M-16 at a monster that isn't there! It varies widely, and that is why I love it.

"The hours and working conditions also vary greatly. Typically, jobs consist of ten-hour days with pleasant working conditions. Sometimes a shoot can be as quick as three hours, and sometimes thirteen. It all depends on what the director is looking for and when he or she sees it.

"I enjoy being involved in the artistic side of life. I love the people who populate the arts. They are intelligent, funny, and varied. Nine to five has never been my style. I languish and fade under fluorescent light…ahhh, but shine a spotlight my way and watch me grow ten feet tall and bulletproof!

"I most enjoy the variety and the opportunity to become a character. I have worked my share of day jobs, and I hated the monotony of them. Fame is not my goal. Riches are not my goal. I simply want to do what I love and get paid for it. That is my dream.

"The only thing I don't like about acting is that there is a lot of classism. If you are on a shoot as a background actor, many do not afford you the level of treatment that featured or lead actors enjoy. It is simply a fact of life. Most actors at a high level do not act snobbish to the lowest-rung actors, but many of the production people do.

"I would advise those interested in this field to study the craft and art of acting as if your life depended upon it. Enjoy life and experience it to the fullest, because good artists bring all their life experiences to their art. Don't let anyone tell you that you are a fool for following your dream. Would you rather be in your rocking chair saying to yourself, 'I wish I had at least tried,' or, 'I gave it my best shot, and had fun along the way?'"

### Meet Mike Matheson

Mike Matheson earned a Bachelor of Science degree in psychology from Lawrence University in Appleton, Wisconsin. He has earned his livelihood as a full-time, freelance voice-over talent since 1985.

"I've always had an outgoing, performing kind of personality, so this profession seemed natural to me," says Matheson. "I've come to understand the fact that what I have is a gift for which I am very appreciative.

"My background includes studying various musical instruments with private teachers—piano, drums, saxophone, guitar. Then I performed in folk groups and rock bands during high school, singing and playing guitar. While attending college, I first worked in radio at a college station, where I learned the basics of on-air work—production, commercial writing, voice-overs, etc. Then I worked as a professional musician (bass, guitar, vocals) performing in clubs throughout the Midwest, playing in folk, rock, jazz, country, and oldies groups. Next I worked in a small-market cable TV station (Janesville, Wisconsin) in every imaginable capacity. These were definitely the dues-paying years. In the two years I was there, I functioned as a talk show host, sports anchor and play-by-play, advertising salesman, commercial producer-writer and voice-over, camera operator, and telethon host. I can only describe this stage of my career as a real eye-opener, a true learning experience. But it gave me a great deal of perspective regarding what was to come.

"I then worked for a small-market radio station as program-director, disc jockey, commercial producer, voice-over. There I did my first freelance work for a handful of clients as commercial writer, producer and voice-over.

"Subsequently I relocated to Indianapolis and worked as a recording engineer in a studio specializing in commercial production. At the same time, I continued to expand my freelance voice-over work. When the freelance income surpassed my salary as an engineer, I decided it was time to step out on my own.

"Today about 90 percent of my work is actually done in Chicago, where I moved in 1988. Actually, my employers are all over the country, but the work itself is done in Chicago recording studios. There are several studios in the Michigan Avenue area of downtown Chicago that do voice-over recording as well as music and video production, all within about a mile radius of the major advertising agencies they serve. I occasionally work in suburban studios in Evanston and Oak Park. In rare instances, when the client cannot travel to Chicago or refuses to do the recording via telephone, I do the recording out of town. However, one of the advantages of living in Chicago is that most out-of-town employers would rather work in Chicago, traveling here, sometimes combining business and pleasure.

"Ironically, what I do is actually very basic. I talk on radio and TV commercials (as well as for industrial films and tapes). My voice is heard over the picture portion of television spots. It's recorded in a studio, after I have been selected (either from a demo tape, audition, previous employment, or word of mouth), and hired, via my agent, by an ad agency that has requested my voice. I read from a script and am directed by the producer or copywriter who has written the script. In the case of television work, I read to a video that has already been assembled—or 'cold' without the picture. My voice, music, and sound effects are then edited to the picture to complete the commercial. Very seldom do I see or hear the finished product when my part of the job is done, either in television or radio, unless I happen to see or hear it on the air. This can be frustrating, and it would be much more satisfying if I could see what I'd contributed to the completed commercial. Then I wouldn't feel so detached from the creative process.

"There really is no typical day for me. Because of that, it is really up to me to give my day-to-day existence some structure and discipline. The need to keep an even keel is, to me, the single most important aspect of my job. That is because of the unstable and volatile nature inherent in this field. There is very little predictability in the amount of work, income, time required, stress level, or personalities involved in my work. That can be both good and bad. The variety can be very stimulating, as well as stressful.

"My work can be extremely lucrative (a definite plus). With some national commercials, as little as eight or ten hours a week in the studio can be sufficient to earn a handsome living. A vast majority pay much less, however, and because of the occasional big payoff, the field is extremely competitive. For that reason, extensive (and expensive) marketing is a must. About 75 to 80 percent of my workweek is spent outside the studio, either doing auditions or promotion and marketing. If I get one job in fifteen or twenty auditions, I'm doing extremely well against the several hundred people competing in the Chicago market. To promote myself I do the following:

1. Send two to three mass mailings a year to twenty-five hundred creatives (writers, producers, creative directors) at ad agencies in about ten midwestern markets. All are custom designed and written, either by me or freelancers I hire. Because agency personnel are constantly changing, updating these mailing lists is an ongoing job.

2. Produce a voice demo tape or CD (it's my resume) annually and send copies to the same twenty-five hundred people. This involves collecting copies of commercials I've done, assembling and editing them into a two-minute sample of my work. I personally finance the production, duplication, and on-stage expenses of the tape as well as the mailers.

3. Pay a personal representative to make visits and calls on my behalf. With the number of voice-overs in the market, keeping contact with potential employers is a must.

"During an average week, I spend up to fifteen hours (maybe seven or eight sessions) in the studio recording and another three or four auditioning. The upside of this, at first glance, is lots of free time. However, I have to be available on a moment's notice during regular work hours (forty to fifty hours a week). My time is my own only until someone needs me for work or an audition.

"Adaptability is an absolutely essential trait, and long-term planning is sometimes impossible. Making good use of free time is very important because I never know when it might end. That time is spent working on promotion and staying informed about my industry by reading trade papers and networking with other voice-overs, producers, recording engineers, etc.

"The pace is hectic and unpredictable. There's a lot of 'hurry up and wait' going on. Some weeks I may have only one audition and no sessions. I must wait and, at the same time, be prepared to be at a session immediately. So it can be slow one minute and very busy the next. Other weeks I may have four sessions on Monday, then nothing until my Friday afternoon audition. In either case, sessions and auditions are very seldom booked more than a day or two ahead of time.

"Depending how busy one is doing sessions and auditions, this career either can be relaxed or stressful. It is most relaxing when there is a slow, but steady, stream of sessions and auditions—a condition that almost never exits! Perhaps the most unsettling part of the job is its unpredictability. Being extremely busy can be hectic and stressful but preferable to, and certainly less stressful than, no work and no income.

"Sessions themselves can also range from a relaxed atmosphere, perhaps with a producer and client you like and know well, to very stressful, with many personalities (writer, producer, account executives, client, engineer, other voice-overs) and egos, many of whom you may even not know are involved. You may have the wrong voice for the job. Or you may be ill. Or you may simply have an off day. You've auditioned and are hired and paid to do well. If you don't, you probably won't work for that producer, agency, or client again. When you have a bad day, it makes them look bad.

"It's hardly ever physically dangerous. The most dangerous thing is if something were to happen to prevent me from working. If I don't work I don't earn. If I became disabled, private disability insurance wouldn't begin to replace my earnings. There are no paid vacations. If I leave town, I might miss work that could potentially pay thousands of dollars. Learning to relax on vacations is a real art. I have to put lost income out of my mind so I can enjoy my time away.

"The other danger is that my voice will somehow go out of style, that whatever people like about it will no longer be in demand. I've accepted that I really have no control over that. I've learned that all I can do is continue to remind people I'm available, give it my best when I'm called, and save my money when the big jobs come along; because as one recording engineer said to me at the end of a recording session, 'you're fired again.' In some ways that sums up my existence as freelance voice-over. Every time I finish a job, I'm unemployed again and in search of the next one.

"When I am hired for a job, I take great satisfaction knowing I've beaten the best in the business to get that job. High risk, high payoff. The financial rewards pale in comparison to the joy I experience doing what I love. I feel blessed to have this job, one I am proud to say I do well. I love what I do. And, in spite of some of the pitfalls, I wouldn't trade it for any job in the world.

"A friend in the voice-over business says he feels like a thief. He fears that earning a living this way might be outlawed. He says that he's sometimes hesitant to answer his door. He's afraid the police may come to arrest him!

"My advice is to keep your seat belt fastened. Keep your shirt on. Keep your sense of humor. Keep your ego in check. Don't take anything personally—especially rejection. Keep your head. And when you make money, keep it. Remember, when you're working, you're making more than anyone in the room. Make their job easy. Make them look good.

"Enjoy it. You're lucky."

## Meet Richard Koz

Rich Koz has spent his entire broadcasting career in the Chicago area. Born in Chicago, he grew up in the northwest suburbs, getting his first taste of broadcasting at WMTH-FM, the high school radio station at Maine East in Park Ridge. While attending Northwestern University, Rich sent comedy material he had written to DJ and television personality, Jerry G. Bishop, who was, at that time, portraying the original *Svengoolie* at Channel 32 in Chicago. Bishop was so impressed by Rich that he took him on as writer/voice talent for *Svengoolie* and later, when *Svengoolie* was canceled in 1973, brought Rich along to WMAQ Radio as producer/writer, second banana on his WMAQ-AM morning show.

"In 1974 I began a three-and-one-half year relationship with comedy legend Dick Orkin, creator of *Chickenman* and *Tooth Fairy* radio serials, and was writer/talent on many of Orkin's radio commercials and features," says Koz. "With Orkin, I co-wrote sixty-five episodes of *Chickenman Returns for the Last Time Again,* which is still syndicated all over the world.

"In the late seventies both Orkin and Jerry G. Bishop (independently) migrated to the West Coast. Before leaving, Bishop gave me permission to do *Son of Svengoolie*—an idea Bishop had originally planned as a vehicle he would produce with me as the next *Svengoolie*—that had never made it past a few false starts.

"With Bishop's blessing I started shopping the idea around and, in June 1979, *Son of Svengoolie* premiered on Channel 32 in Chicago. It ran for six and one-half years, winning three consecutive Chicago Emmy Awards for Best Entertainment Series.

"Channel 32 canceled *Son of Svengoolie* in January 1986. In the meantime, I freelanced as a commercial talent/writer and was a fill-in radio host on WGN radio. Briefly, I was also weekend morning host on The Satellite Music Network's adult-contemporary format, heard all over the world.

"In 1989 I returned to Channel 32, hosting late movies as myself and other characters. The show's premise was that I was a pirate-broadcaster breaking into the station's signal to do his comedy bits. The premise was so convincing that its promos brought calls from viewers—and even the FCC—asking about the 'mysterious interruptions.' The show won me an additional Chicago Emmy as Best Entertainment Series.

"At the same time, I was morning host on WCKG-FM, broadcasting live from such unique places as Disney/MGM Studios in Orlando and Jamaica and sharing the mike with Paul Schaeffer, Jerry—The Beaver—Mathers, and stars of *My Three Sons*. In 1990 I became daily host for all the Channel 32 kids programming, later adding additional duties as weekend weatherman and host for live events like Taste of Chicago, and New Years Eve broadcasts.

"After leaving Channel 32 in 1993, and another round of freelancing, I joined General Manager Neal Sabin in bringing WCIU on the air at The U—a mainstream independent TV station. No longer *Son of Svengoolie,* my mentor, Jerry G. Bishop declared me all grown up. I brought the station on the air as Svengoolie himself!

"I now portray the popular character each week on The U with his cast of Doug Graves, the laid-back musical sidekick, and Tombstone, the talking skull. I continue to popularize rubber chickens, bad movies, and the local suburb of Berwyn. In addition to the popular musical numbers and commercial parodies *Svengoolie* has always been known for, each show features a segment of the movie produced in 'Svensurround,' with new sound effects, dubbed-in dialogue, and visuals. This technique was first done by both me and Bishop in the 1970s before the advent of *Mystery Science Theatre 3000*. Svengoolie's hard work and comic genius keeps paying off. 'Svengoolie—The First Year,' a look back at *Svengoolie's* first year on WCIU, was rewarded with a Chicago Emmy for Best Entertainment Program-Special.

"I also appear on Channel 26 as myself and various other characters—whatever is needed. I am involved in many aspects of the station, both on-screen and off, and am proud to be part of one of Chicago's most creative stations, Channel 26—The U.

"As far as the *Svengoolie* program goes, a typical week begins with my screening the movie for the show we're working on that week—dividing it into the proper number of segments, editing it down to time and sometimes for content, and taking notes on the film on which to base my comedy bits in the show. During this same time, I'm working on the postproduction of the previous week's show, adding and editing production elements to make the finished program. Then I write the bits for the show, while consulting with my musician sidekick, Doug Scharf, about what song we'll do a parody of that week, for which he creates a complete musical track in his studio. I also work with assistants to get the necessary props, costumes, and production elements we need. We then tape all the show elements, usually on Thursday. On Friday I get together all necessary elements for the postproduction that starts the next week.

"At the same time, I work on promos, specials, regular station voice-over work, and writing and do public appearances as Svengoolie. This television station is unusual in that it is a smaller, family-owned station in such a major market. It is doubtful that I would get to do so much, and wear so many different hats, at any other station in a market this size. It is extremely hectic, with the added pressure of trying to get good ratings. I often end up working at home as well, and doing extra appearances on radio and in other media. I put in well over forty hours a week between home and the workplace. The work atmosphere is like a beehive, but very conducive to creativity. There are many people all contributing in various ways to the creative process that produces the finished product, so that there is a sense of community and camaraderie. I am fortunate to work with many people, directors, and technical staff who like what we do enough to do more than is expected of them. I take it as a personal compliment that they want my stuff to be the best it can possibly be!

"What I like best is the satisfaction of creating good, funny material that keeps people entertained—quality stuff that people remember and want more of (just as I mentioned that it was people's fond memories that made me do the character again). I also like the fact that I have so much hands-on creative control over what I do.

"The downside is the lack of privacy. People do recognize me, and I am aware of the possible dangers to my family from people who find out where we live. Also, the work can eat into time with my family. I find it hard to complain, though. There have been stretches with less work, and I'd rather be overworked and providing for my family than having loads of free time and more money going out each month than there is coming in!

"My advice is to have a realistic view of the business. It is very tough and competitive, and you really need to want to be doing this kind of stuff to survive the pressures of living and dying by ratings, the whims of management, changes in format, etc. The key to survival is adaptability and being able to do as many different things as possible.

"Also, don't think you can do as I did and send me material and I'll hire you and you'll become grandson or granddaughter of Svengoole. I still have no problem coming up with my own material, and the Sven family line will end with me!"

### Meet Joe Hansard

Auditioning for a television commercial at the age of five was enough for Joe Hansard to become hooked, and he currently works as an actor and a stand-up comedian in New York City. He attended trade school at the Broadcasting Institute of Maryland and has also been an actor-in-residence at the International Film & Television Workshops. Other training includes Stand-Up New York (comedian school) and the Mike Fenton Scene Study Workshop for Film. He has performed his comedy routine at several comedy clubs in New York, and his favorite acting credit is the part of Jimmy Lee Shields in the pilot episode of *Homicide.*

"I've always had a fascination for the motion picture industry," Hansard says. "I enjoy the camaraderie and collaboration that comes with a film or television project, as well as the challenges. I liken it to being in a football game, where you are given the ball and you run with it. As an actor, I try to expand on the ideas given me by bringing my own uniqueness to a role.

"I like surrounding myself with creative, enthusiastic, and energetic people. There is nothing better than working with folks who truly love their work and get excited about what they do. As a stand-up comedian, nothing is more exhilarating than laughter and applause. It is sweeter than any candy, and it doesn't rot my teeth!

"I owe everything to my mom and dad. I performed at talent showcases in elementary school and was into magic tricks in my preteens. After high school I didn't know what I wanted to do with my life, and mom came to the rescue again by suggesting a trade school for broadcasting. I was about nineteen or twenty when I landed my first paying gig as a DJ for an AM radio station in the college town of Shippensburg, Pennsylvania.

"I got my SAG card when director Christopher Leitch cast me in a principal role in the feature film *The Hitter,* starring Ron O'Neal and Adolph Caesar (who was an Oscar winner for *A Soldier's Story*).

"I moved to Los Angeles in the early 1980s and had an absolutely horrible experience there. I couldn't get work, had my car repossessed, went bankrupt, and was in poor shape emotionally. It was the darkest time of my life, and there seemed to be no light at the end of the tunnel. But I finally got my act together and moved back east, and that's when Barry Levinson cast me in the pilot episode of *Homicide* on NBC. The 'Gone for Goode' episode that I appear in aired after the Superbowl in 1993 and was the highest-rated *Homicide* episode ever.

"I decided to pursue stand-up comedy as a means to network and get myself out there. So far I have performed at Stand-Up New York, The Comedy Store, and The Fun Factory.

"The bulk of my typical day is actually spent looking for work. I track casting leads wherever I can find them, either through personal contacts with the industry professionals I've been associated with over the years, via the Internet, or just the good old grapevine. This is a crazy business. Sometimes it's busy and full beyond belief, and there's barely time to catch my breath. At other times, weeks and even months can go by with nary a job in sight.

"If I'm working on a film or television show, the days are very long, between ten and fourteen hours a day. There is either a real camaraderie that forms on a set, or a real paranoia, depending on any number of circumstances and variables in or out of your control that are inherent to the industry. In most cases it is quite enjoyable, as cast and crew are very professional and you, more often than not, will get kudos when the director or producer likes the work you are doing. I've found that the entire production and creative team literally evolves into a family.

"I like to work! I love meeting and working with creative, talented actors and directors. I love the business and wouldn't trade it for anything! But the thing I like least is not having any work, having to sit idle. I see an acting coach once a week and take classes to stay tuned up.

"The most important thing is to love your work. Know that there is much competition and some lean times, but always remember to enjoy what you do and have fun doing it!"

## FOR MORE INFORMATION

Information about opportunities in regional theaters may be obtained from:

Theatre Communications Group, Inc.
  355 Lexington Avenue
  New York, NY 10017

A directory of theatrical programs may be purchased from:

National Association of Schools of Theatre
11250 Roger Bacon Drive, Suite 21
Reston, VA 22090

Additional information may be secured from the following associations:

Actors' Equity Association
165 West Forty-Sixth Street
New York, NY 10036

Alliance of Canadian Cinema
Television and Radio Artists
2239 Yonge Street
Toronto, Ontario
Canada M5S 2B5

Alliance of Resident Theaters/
New York
325 Spring Street
New York, NY 10013

American Federation of Television
and Radio Artists (AFTRA)
260 Madison Avenue
New York, NY 10016

American Film Institute
P.O. Box 27999
2021 North Western Avenue
Los Angeles, CA 90027

American Guild of Variety Artists
(AGVA)
184 Fifth Avenue
New York, NY 10019

American Theater Association (ATA)
1010 Wisconsin Avenue NW
Washington, DC 20007

American Theatre Works, Inc.
Theatre Directories
P.O. Box 519
Dorset, VT 05251

Canadian Actors' Equity Association
260 Richmond Street East
Toronto, Ontario
Canada M5A 1P4

National Arts Jobbank
141 East Palace Avenue
Santa Fe, NM 87501

National Association of Schools of
Theatre
11250 Roger Bacon Drive, Suite 21
Reston, VA 22090

Screen Actors Guild (SAG)
5757 Wilshire Boulevard
Los Angeles, CA 90036

Theater Communications Group, Inc.
355 Lexington Avenue
New York, NY 10017

More information on this field can be found in the following books:

Bjorguine Bekken, Bonnie. *Opportunities in Performing Arts.* Lincolnwood, IL:
NTC/Contemporary Publishing Group, Inc., 1991.
Moore, Dick. *Opportunities in Acting.* Lincolnwood, IL: NTC/Contemporary
Publishing Group, Inc., 1993.

## CHAPTER 2

# CAREERS IN MUSIC AND DANCE

> When music fails to agree to the ear, to soothe the ear and the heart and
> the senses, then it has missed its point.
>
> —Maria Callas

Arthur Rubinstein learned the names of the piano keys by the time he
was two years old. Ray Charles began to play the piano at age three.
Yehudi Menuhin performed solos with the San Francisco Symphony
Orchestra at the age of seven. Buddy Holly won $5.00 singing "Down the
River of Memories" at a talent show at five. Gladys Knight won $2,000
singing on the Ted Mack's Amateur Hour at age seven. Marvin Hamlisch
was accepted at the Juilliard School of Music at age seven. All of these
musical geniuses got their starts very early as those who choose careers in
music and dance often do.

## MUSICIANS

About 256,000 musicians perform in the United States. Included in this
number are those who play in any one of thirty-nine regional, ninty metropolitan, or thirty major symphony orchestras. (Large orchestras employ
from 85 to 105 musicians, while smaller ones employ 60 to 75 players.)
Also counted are those who are a part of hundreds of small orchestras, symphony orchestras, pop and jazz groups, and those who broadcast or record.

Instrumental musicians may play a variety of musical instruments in an
orchestra, popular band, marching band, military band, concert band,
symphony, dance band, rock group, or jazz group and may specialize in

string, brass, woodwind, or percussion instruments or electronic synthe-sizers. A large percentage of musicians are proficient in playing several related instruments, such as the flute and clarinet. (This increases employ-ment opportunities.) Those who are very talented have the option to per-form as soloists.

Rehearsing and performing take up much of musicians' time and energy. In addition, musicians, especially those without agents, may need to perform a number of other routine tasks such as: making reservations, keeping track of auditions and/or recordings, arranging for sound effects amplifiers and other equipment to enhance performances, designing light-ing and costumes, doing makeup, keeping the books, and setting up adver-tising, concerts, tickets, programs, and contracts. Musicians also need to plan the sequence of the numbers to be performed and/or arrange their music according to the conductor's instructions before performances.

Musicians also must keep their instruments clean, polished, tuned, and in proper working order. In addition they are expected to attend meetings with agents, employers, and conductors or directors to discuss contracts, engagements, and any other business activities.

Performing musicians encompass a wide variety of careers. Here are just a few of the possibilities:

### Session Musician

The session musician is the one responsible for playing background music in a studio while a recording artist is singing. The session musician may also be called a freelance musician, backup musician, session player, or studio musician. Session musicians are used for all kinds of recordings, Broadway musicals, operas, rock and folk songs, and pop tunes.

Versatility is the most important ingredient for these professionals; the more instruments the musician has mastered, the greater number of musi-cal styles he or she can offer, the more possibilities for musical assign-ments. Session musicians often are listed through contractors who call upon them when the need arises. Other possibilities exist through direct requests made by the artists themselves, the group members, or the man-agement team.

The ability to sight-read is important for all musicians, but it is particu-larly crucial for session musicians. Rehearsal time is usually very limited, and costs make it too expensive to have to do retakes.

## Section Leader–Section Member

Section members are the individuals who play instruments in an orchestra. They must be talented at playing their instrument of choice and able to learn the music on their own. Rehearsals are strictly designed for putting all of the instruments and individuals together and for establishing cues such as phrasing and correct breathing. It is expected that all musicians practice sufficiently on their own before rehearsals.

## Concertmaster/Concertmistress

Those chosen to be concertmasters or concertmistresses have the important responsibility of leading the string sections of the orchestras during both rehearsals and concerts. In addition, these individuals are responsible for tuning the rest of the orchestra. This is the "music" you hear for about fifteen to twenty seconds before the musicians begin to play their first piece.

Concertmasters and concertmistresses must possess leadership abilities and be very knowledgeable of both the music and all the instruments. They answer directly to the conductor.

## Floor Show Band Member

Musicians who belong to bands that perform floor shows appear in hotels, nightclubs, cruise ships, bars, concert arenas, and cafes. Usually the bands do two shows per night with a particular number of sets in each show. Additionally they may be required to play one or two dance sets during the course of the engagement. The audience is seated during the shows and gets up to dance during the dance sets. Shows may include costuming, dialogue, singing, jokes, skits, unusual sound effects, and anything else the band decides to include. Floor show bands may be contracted to appear in one place for one night or several weeks at a time. As expected, a lot of traveling is involved for those who take up this career.

## Choir Director/Church or Temple Musician

Choir directors are responsible for recruiting and directing choirs and planning the music programs. They are often given the job of auditioning potential members of the choir, setting up rehearsal schedules, overseeing and directing them, and choosing the music. They may be in charge of the church's or temple's music library or may designate another individual to do so. Working closely with the minister or other religious leader of the congregation, choir directors plan all concerts, programs, and other musical events.

In addition choir directors develop and maintain the music budgets for their religious institutions. In some cases choral directors are expected to maintain office hours each week. During those times, individuals may write music, handle administrative chores, or work with small groups of singers and/or the organist.

Usually a bachelor's degree in church music is required; often a master's degree is requested.

### Organist

Organists play their instruments at religious and special services like weddings and funerals. Recitals also may be given as part of the congregation's spiritual programming. Organists choose the music to be played or may work with the choir or music director to accomplish this task. Organists also are responsible for making sure organs are in proper working order and may advise the congregation on other music-related issues. Sometimes the organist is also the choir director.

### Conductor and Choral Director

The music conductor is the director for all of the performers in a musical presentation, whether it be singing or instrumental. Though there are many types of conductors—symphony, choral groups, dance bands, opera, marching bands, and ballet—in all cases the music conductor is the one who is in charge of interpreting the music.

Conductors audition and select musicians, choose the music to accommodate the talents and abilities of the musicians, and direct rehearsals and performances, applying conducting techniques to achieve desired musical effects like harmony, rhythm, tempo, and shading.

Orchestral conductors lead instrumental music groups, such as orchestras, dance bands, and various popular ensembles. Choral directors lead choirs and glee clubs, sometimes working with a band or orchestra conductor.

### Announcer/Disc Jockey

Announcers play an important role in keeping listeners tuned into a radio or television station. They are the ones who must read messages, commercials, and scripts in an entertaining, interesting, and/or enlightening way. They are also responsible for introducing station breaks, perhaps interviewing guests, and selling commercial time to advertisers. Sometimes they are called disc jockeys, but actually disc jockeys are the announcers who oversee musical programming at radio stations and during parties, dances, and other special occasions.

Disc jockeys also may interview guests and make public service announcements, announce the time, do the weather forecast, or even report the news. They must be very knowledgeable about music in general and all aspects of their specialties, specifically the music and the groups who play and/or sing that kind of music. Their programs may feature general music, rock, pop, country and western, or any specific musical period or style such as tunes from the 1950s or 1960s.

Since radio programs are usually performed live, disc jockeys must be quick thinking and personable. Most often they do not have a written script from which to read. They must be able to perform well under stress and in situations where things do not go as planned. Thus the best disc jockeys possess pleasant, soothing voices and good wit and are able to keep listeners fully entertained.

It takes considerable skills to work the radio controls, read reports, watch the clock, select music, talk with someone, and be entertaining to the audience, all at the same time.

### DANCERS

Ever since ancient times, dancers have expressed ideas, stories, rhythm, and sound with their bodies. In addition to being an art form for its own sake, dance also complements opera, musical comedy, television, movies, music videos, and commercials. Therefore, many dancers sing and act as well as dance.

Dancers most often perform as a group, although a few top artists dance solo. Many dancers combine stage work with teaching or choreography. Here are some examples of dance specialties:

## Choreographers

Choreographers create original dances. They also may create new interpretations to traditional dances like the ballet, "Nutcracker," since few dances are written down. Choreographers instruct performers at rehearsals to achieve the desired effect. They also audition performers.

## Ballet Dancers

Ballet dancing requires a lot of training—in fact, more than any other kind of dancing. Ballet dancers are performers who express a theme or story.

## Modern Dancers

Modern dancers use bodily movements and facial expressions to express ideas and moods. Jazz is an example of a modern dance.

## Tap Dancers

Tap dancers use tap shoes to keep in time with all kinds of music. The shoes allow them to tap our various dance rhythms.

## The Life of a Dancer

Dancing is strenuous. Rehearsals require very long hours and usually take place daily, including weekends and holidays. For shows on the road, weekend travel is often necessary. Rehearsals and practice are generally scheduled during the day. Since most performances take place in the evening, dancers must usually work late hours.

Due to the physical demands, most dancers stop performing by their late thirties, but they sometimes continue to work in the dance field as choreographers, dance teachers and coaches, or as artistic directors. Some celebrated dancers, however, continue performing beyond the age of fifty.

Dancers work in a variety of settings, including eating and drinking establishments, theatrical and television productions, dance studios and schools, dance companies and bands, and amusement parks.

In addition there are many dance instructors in secondary schools, colleges and universities, and private studios. Many teachers also perform from time to time.

New York City is the home of many of the major dance companies. Other cities with full-time professional dance companies include Atlanta, Boston, Chicago, Cincinnati, Cleveland, Columbus, Dallas, Houston, Miami, Milwaukee, Philadelphia, Pittsburgh, Salt Lake City, San Francisco, Seattle, and Washington, DC.

## TRAINING FOR MUSICIANS

Many people who become professional musicians begin studying an instrument at an early age. They may gain valuable experience playing in a school or community band or orchestra or with a group of friends. Singers usually start training when their voices mature. Participation in school musicals or in a choir often provides good early training and experience.

Musicians need extensive and prolonged training to acquire the necessary skill, knowledge, and ability to interpret music. This training may be obtained through private study with an accomplished musician, in a college or university music program, in a music conservatory, or through practice with a group. For study in an institution, an audition frequently is necessary. Formal courses include musical theory, music interpretation, composition, conducting, and instrumental and voice instruction.

Composers, conductors, and arrangers need advanced training in these subjects as well.

Many colleges, universities, and music conservatories grant bachelor's or higher degrees in music. Many also grant degrees in music education to qualify graduates for a state certificate to teach music in an elementary or secondary school.

Those who perform popular music must have an understanding of, and feeling for, the style of music that interests them, but classical training can expand their employment opportunities, as well as their musical abilities.

Although voice training is an asset for singers of popular music, many with untrained voices have successful careers. As a rule, musicians take lessons with private teachers when young and seize every opportunity to make amateur or professional appearances.

### Desirable Personal Qualities

Young people who are considering careers in music should have musical talent, versatility, creative ability, poise, and the stage presence to face large audiences.

Since quality performance requires constant study and practice, self-discipline is vital. Moreover, musicians who play concert and nightclub engagements must have physical stamina because frequent travel and night performances are required. They also must be prepared to face the anxiety of intermittent employment and rejections when auditioning for work.

## TRAINING FOR DANCERS

Training for dancers varies according to the type of dance. Early ballet training for women usually begins at five to eight years of age and is often given by private teachers and independent ballet schools. Serious training traditionally begins between the ages of ten and twelve. Men often begin their training between the ages of ten and fifteen.

Students who demonstrate potential in the early teens receive more intensive and advanced professional training at regional ballet schools or schools conducted under the auspices of the major ballet companies.

Leading dance school companies often have summer training programs from which they select candidates for admission to their regular full-time training program. Most dancers have their professional auditions by age seventeen or eighteen; however, training and practice never end. Professional ballet dancers have one to one and one-half hours of lessons every day and spend many additional hours practicing and rehearsing.

Early and intensive training also is important for the modern dancer, but modern dance generally does not require as many years of training as ballet. Because of the strenuous and time-consuming training required, a dancer's formal academic instruction may be minimal. However, a broad, general education including music, literature, history, and the visual arts is helpful in the interpretation of dramatic episodes, ideas, and feelings.

Many colleges and universities offer bachelor's or higher degrees in dance. This might be through the departments of music, physical education, fine arts, or theater. Most programs concentrate on modern dance, but also offer courses in ballet/classical techniques, dance composition, dance history, dance criticism, and movement analysis.

A college education is not essential to obtaining employment as a professional dancer. In fact, ballet dancers who postpone their first audition until graduation may compete at a disadvantage with younger dancers. On the other hand, a college degree can help the dancer who retires at an early age—as often happens—and wishes to enter another field of work.

Completion of a college program in dance and education is essential to qualify for employment as a college or elementary/high school dance teacher. Colleges, as well as conservatories, generally require graduate degrees, but performance experience often may be substituted. However, a college background is not necessary for teaching dance or choreography professionally. Studio schools usually require teachers to have experience as performers.

## JOB OUTLOOK FOR MUSICIANS

Competition for musician jobs is keen, and talent alone is no guarantee of success. The glamour and potentially high earnings in this occupation attract many talented individuals.

Still, overall, employment of musicians is expected to grow faster than the average for all occupations through the year 2005. Almost all new wage and salary jobs for musicians will arise in religious organizations and bands, orchestras, and other entertainment groups. A decline in employment is projected for salaried musicians in restaurants and bars, although they comprise a very small proportion of all salaried musicians. Bars, which regularly employ musicians, are expected to grow more slowly than eating establishments because consumption of alcoholic beverages outside the home is expected to continue to decline. The fastest-growing segment of restaurants is the moderately priced, family dining restaurants, which seldom provide live entertainment to their customers. Overall, most job openings for musicians will arise from the need to replace those who leave the field each year because they are unable to make a living solely as musicians.

## JOB OUTLOOK FOR DANCERS

Dancers and choreographers face very keen competition for jobs. The number of applicants will continue to exceed the number of job openings, and only the most talented will find regular employment.

Employment of dancers and choreographers is expected to grow faster than the average for all occupations through the year 2005 due to the public's continued interest in this form of artistic expression. However, cuts in funding for the National Endowment for the Arts and related organizations could adversely affect employment in this field. Although jobs will rise each year due to increased demand, most job openings will occur as dancers and choreographers retire and leave the occupation for other reasons, and as dance companies search for and find outstanding talent.

The best job opportunities are expected to be with national dance companies because of the demand for performances outside of New York City. Opera companies also will provide some employment opportunities. Dance groups affiliated with colleges and universities and television and motion pictures will offer some opportunities. Moreover, the growing popularity of dance in recent years has resulted in increased employment opportunities in teaching dance.

With innovations such as electronic sounds and music videos, choreography is becoming a more challenging field of endeavor and will offer some employment opportunities for highly talented and creative individuals.

## SALARIES FOR MUSICIANS

Earnings for musicians often depend on a performer's professional reputation, place of employment, and the number of hours worked. The most successful musicians can earn far more than the minimum salaries indicated below.

According to the American Federation of Musicians, minimum salaries in major orchestras range from about $1,000 to $1,200 per week during the performing season. Each orchestra works out a separate contract with its members. The season of these top orchestras ranges from forty-eight to fifty-two weeks, with most being fifty-two weeks. In regional orchestras, the minimum salaries are between $400 and $700 per week, and the seasons last twenty-five to thirty-eight weeks, with an average of thirty weeks. Some now work a fifty-two-week season. Community orchestras, however, have more limited levels of funding and offer salaries that are much lower for seasons of shorter duration.

Musicians employed in motion picture or television recording and those employed by recording companies are paid a minimum ranging from about $200 to $260 a week, depending on the size of the ensemble. Musicians employed by some symphony orchestras work under master wage agreements, which guarantee a season's work up to fifty-two weeks. Many other musicians may face relatively long periods of unemployment between jobs. Even when employed, however, many work part-time. Thus, their earnings generally are lower than those in many other occupations. Moreover, since they may not work steadily for one employer, some performers cannot qualify for unemployment compensation, and few have either sick leave or vacations with pay. For these reasons, many musicians give private lessons or take jobs unrelated to music to supplement their earnings as performers.

Many musicians belong to a local of the American Federation of Musicians. Professional singers usually belong to a branch of the Associated Actors and Artists of America.

## SALARIES FOR DANCERS

The earnings for many professional dancers are governed by union contracts. Dancers in major opera ballets, classical ballet, and modern dance corps belong to the American Guild of Musical Artists, Inc., AFL-CIO. Those on live or videotaped television belong to the American Federation of Television and Radio Artists. Those who perform in films and on television belong to the Screen Actors Guild or the Screen Extras Guild. Those in musical comedies are members of the Actors' Equity Association. The unions and producers sign basic agreements specifying minimum salary rates, hours of work, benefits, and other conditions of employment. However, the contract each dancer signs with the producer of the show may be more favorable than the basic agreement.

The minimum weekly salary for dancers in ballet and modern productions is about $610. According to the American Guild of Musical Artists, new first-year dancers being paid for single performances under a union agreement earn about $475 per week and $70 per rehearsal hour. Dancers on tour receive an additional allowance for room and board. The minimum performance rate for dancers in theatrical motion pictures is about $100 per day of filming. The normal workweek is thirty hours including rehearsals and matinee and evening performances, but it may be longer. Extra compensation is paid for additional hours worked.

Earnings from dancing are generally low because dancers' employment is irregular. They often must supplement their income by taking temporary jobs unrelated to dancing.

Dancers covered by union contracts are entitled to some paid sick leave, paid vacations, and various health and pension benefits, including extended sick pay and childbirth provisions, provided by their unions. Employers contribute toward these benefits. Most other dancers do not receive any benefits.

Earnings of choreographers vary greatly. Earnings from fees and performance royalties range from about $970 a week in small professional theaters, to more than $30,000 for an eight-to-ten week rehearsal period for a Broadway production. In high budget films, choreographers make $3,000 for a five-day week; in television, $7,500 to $10,000 for up to fourteen workdays.

## PROFILES

### Meet Mark Marek

Mark Marek is a singer and the owner of Private Stock Variety Dance Band of Lenexa, Kansas. His background includes two years of college with course work focusing on music theory, audio and engineering, and the fundamentals of music and business.

"I started playing the drums in junior high school and then learned how to play the six string guitar," says Marek. "By the time I was sixteen, my brother had his own band, so I started playing and learning about bands from him. Fourteen years ago, I started my own band.

"My band is primarily a country club/high-dollar type band. We play mostly at weddings, country clubs, and other formal occasions. The band's working hours are usually 6:30 P.M. until 1:00 A.M., mostly on Fridays and Saturdays. Most gigs usually last three to four hours and we have to arrive there at least an hour and a half before the start time. We generally do one-hour sets, with a twenty minute break every hour or so. In addition to setting up, we also have to break down the equipment. Because we've been together for so long, we don't need to rehearse much, perhaps every three to four months.

"I love seeing the reaction of the audience. It's fun to know and see that they are having a good time. That's the thrill I get out of it. What I least like is the inconsistency in bookings. Each month the number of gigs changes, which affects the cash flow. The peak periods for the band are December and May through June.

"During the week, I mostly take bookings, spend time on the phone getting the specifics for each one, and contact the five band members about our schedule. I also handle all of the contracts for each performance. Aside from the band, I also give private guitar lessons and book gigs for other bands.

"To approach success in the music industry, you need to have good people skills, a general sense of business, a real enjoyment for what you do, a recognition of what your niche is in the music world, patience, good customer relations skills, expert technical skills, and a knowledge of audio and video.

"Having a band is a business, not an ego trip. You really need to have a basic knowledge of business and marketing. You can be the best musician, but you have to know how to sell yourself in order to be successful. It's a tough way to make a living—that's why you have to really have a passion for the business."

### Meet Ed Goeke

Ed Goeke is the Music Director of Christ Episcopal Church in Overland Park, Kansas. He has a Bachelor of Arts degree and a Master of Arts degree in music education from the University of Iowa, in addition to a Master of Arts degree from the University of Kansas in Lawrence, Kansas, where he is a Ph.D. candidate in music education.

"I studied voice, piano, and French horn from the time I was in junior high school," says Goeke. "Both of my parents are music educators, so it was a natural thing for me to enter a career in music. Music has affected my whole life. It *is* my life. I can't imagine not having musical outlets. I will probably never leave music. What I find most gratifying is performing well, knowing that people are grateful for a job well done.

"Sunday is the culmination of the work I do all week. The day starts around 8:00 A.M. with warm-up for the first service, which is at 8:45 A.M. Those involved include an ensemble of eight to ten people. When this service is over, then rehearsal starts—9:30 or so—for the 10:45 service. This is a choir of twenty-four people with an organist. The service is over around noon. There is a break for lunch, then around 2:30 rehearsal starts for the 5:30 service. We organize and plan for the next week's selection. The day usually ends around 7:00 P.M.

"Its very casual here in terms of dress and chain of command. A lot of time is spent in rehearsal and planning for worship services. The busiest time is the whole month of December due to the number of liturgies and the importance of the spiritual services.

"I took this job because it enables me to use my classical background and work in a traditional setting, but at the same time I lead others in contemporary music. I can work with a variety of musicians. It's great working with this fine group of people. I like working with a mission in mind—having a goal of bringing people closer to God through worship by providing windows of opportunity through excellent music. The music allows people to participate more actively by providing a means that inspires/moves people more deeply to developing a closer relationship with God. What I like least is reproducing music and having to stay on top of all of the paperwork.

"Church jobs are changing dramatically. The best way to be equipped is to get very good at one thing. If you want to be a music director of a church full-time, then it is important to have excellent keyboarding skills. I'd recommend gaining skills in arranging and improvisational skills and exposure to a wide variety of music. It is important to be able to work well with people. This can be accomplished by performing in church choirs and acquiring experience.

"It's important that you are a people person, that you are a team builder/consensus builder, that you are sensitive to people's needs, that you have a thorough knowledge of what makes music good, and that you have a background in performance. Pluses also include good knowledge of literature for choirs, a background in liturgy, the ability to take available resources and arrange on the spot, good improvisational skills, the ability to communicate effectively, and good organizational skills."

## Meet Priscilla Gale

Soprano Priscilla Gale attended both the Juilliard School of Music and the Cleveland Institute of Music. She also has studied in Austria and with private teachers Luigi Ricci (in Rome) and Michael Trimble. Currently, when she's not performing with an opera company or symphony orchestra, she is a faculty member at Wesleyan University in Middletown, Connecticut, where she teaches voice.

"Having come from a very musical family of pianists, singers, and violinists, I was at the piano at the age of five," says Gale. "My family always assumed that I would pursue a career as a pianist, but I realized my real joy and fulfillment was in singing, not the piano. As I began to explore that world more thoroughly, I discovered opera, and I found my home. The rest is history. I received my first professional contract with the Ft. Wayne (Indiana) Symphony Orchestra during my senior year at Cleveland Institute of Music.

"Every engagement you experience changes you in the most wonderful way. You, as an artist, grow on multiple levels, personally—inwardly and artistically—outwardly, and one thing leads to another. Each time, your life as an artist is changed; you grow in some immeasurable, wonderful way, and the possibilities are limitless.

"No one job site is like another. In opera the rehearsals are intense, with the appropriate union breaks, but with long, long days, usually over a ten-to-twelve hour period daily, and over two weeks, or perhaps three. It really depends on how a company works, and they all work differently.

"Orchestra jobs tend to be over a three- or four-day period. Usually you have a piano rehearsal with the conductor, then there are one or two orchestra rehearsals, followed by the performances. It is always busy and intense, but exciting. It is fast paced, and one must know one's craft. There is little room for poor preparation. And, you must always have the ability to adjust to every circumstance and environment, for no two are ever the same. Every conductor is different, every director, etc. You must be very adaptable and professional.

"What I love most about my work is the ability to touch an audience— people I never meet individually, but collectively. My heart and soul meet theirs. But there are just not enough performance opportunities for every-one, and it is no longer possible to make a full-time living at this career, unless you are one of the lucky top 20 percent.

"I always tell people who want to do this kind of work to look inward and ask if there is anything else in life that will bring them happiness and fulfillment. If so, then I suggest that they do that instead. If not, then they should by all means pursue this career. But know that it is—especially in the beginning—a very complicated business that represents a difficult life.

"Talent is but a small piece of it. Most people cannot comprehend the level of sacrifice that this career requires. There is that wonderful, roman-tic notion of being the starving artist, but there's nothing romantic about it when you're living it.

"However, with hard work, determination, perseverance, and an unwa-vering faith in yourself, anything can happen. The journey is an incredible ride and one I would not have missed. And as I look back on my past, on my present, and toward my future, I can honestly say that I am one of the lucky ones."

## Meet Karen Tyler

Karen Tyler of Austin, Texas, earned an Associate of Arts degree from Pepperdine University. She has been working as a blues singer/song-writer/guitarist since 1979.

"I had a natural talent for singing and found songwriting to be an incredible emotional outlet," says Tyler. "And I have developed some pretty good business skills in order to stay in the music business. From the beginning, being front and center stage and being appreciated for my 'feelings' was important to me.

"Many artists have to have day jobs to support their music, making it very difficult to actually have the time to write, record, and do live performances. My husband and I moved to Texas so that we could afford to live on one salary while I pursued my music. Since he is also my bass player, my studio engineer/producer, and maker and repairer of guitars, he, of course, benefits from any of my successes.

"I get up fairly early each day and start to work by 9:00 or 10:00 A.M.," she says. "I have so many tasks to accomplish! I keep a mailing list and create all of my own promotional materials via the computer and a couple of printers. I am responsible for all of the bookkeeping and accounting of band income and CD and tape sales. I write a quarterly newsletter. I also make demo tapes and mail out promotional packages almost constantly. I do tons of research on radio stations, booking agents, clubs, festivals, record companies, and the like. I read everything I can get my hands on about the music business and the blues. I spend anywhere from one to four hours a day doing just the business of music. In addition I play several nights a week from two to four hours sometimes traveling three and four hours to play. Nothing at all may happen for a period of time, and just when I get into a routine I really like, someone will call or an opportunity will arise that will take all of my attention.

"There is never a time when something like songwriting or practicing guitar doesn't take a backseat to some kind of business duty. I have tried to get a manager but have had some really bad experiences, and at this point in my career, I feel that it is better if I retain the control of my career even if the responsibilities are a bit overwhelming. Everyone always has a suggestion about what you should be doing to help your career. And you can't possibly do everything people suggest, so making an action plan and sticking to it is the best thing. Trying to be organized is my biggest challenge and getting things down on paper helps.

"I spend anywhere from twenty-five to thirty hours a week doing music business and play anywhere from four to twelve hours a week. I work from a home office and so it gets a little lonely. My husband is moving his office into our home, which I assume will make it a bit better for me. At least I will have someone to bounce some ideas off of. Sometimes I really feel like I'm out there all alone.

"I enjoy a good crowd response to my music. It makes it all worthwhile when someone comes up and tells me I have an amazing voice or that I play the guitar well or that a certain song really touched them. The worst part is probably that people don't go out as much as they used to. They are programmed by television, radio, and print media as to what to buy and what to listen to or go to see. They get comfortable going to hear certain acts, and until they have heard rave reviews about someone forty or fifty times, they don't make the effort to go and see them. Even when they do, they are liable to slip back into the habit of going where they always go. A side effect is that talent doesn't count as much as who you know and how much fun you are to hang out with.

"On top of that, bands who want to make it are expected to finance their own recordings, put out expensive CDs, and sell literally thousands of them before a record company will consider signing them. This is kind of hard when you are playing for fewer and fewer people every day.

"I would advise those interested in this career to go to college and develop a talent (preferably nonmusical) whereby you can create your own business: computers, catering, consulting (it really doesn't have to start with a 'C,' though). You have to have some way of supporting yourself and coming up with \$5,000 to \$10,000 every year or two for a CD, and you have to have a flexible schedule so that you can tour and support the CD and work whenever you can."

### Meet Kathryn Maffei

Kathryn Maffei has been playing the piano for more than forty years. She has ten years of classical training through a concert pianist. "When I started taking piano lessons at eight years old," says Maffei, "I began to entertain my family. Then I performed for family and friends' parties, as well as local club and organization events. Quickly it spread to playing the piano for chorus classes in grammar school and high school and for bands and entertaining for many different kinds of local events such as proms, fashion shows, variety shows, plays, and other social functions.

"I got married and took a few years off to raise my family. When my children were of preschool and kindergarten age, I went to school with them and did music classes for their teachers because they did not play the piano or have live music for their classes. I became the church organist in communities in which we lived, and played for weddings, funerals, and masses.

"Once I was heard by others, it quickly spread to doing events at hotels and country clubs and Christmas parties, birthday parties, anniversaries, class reunions, etc. I became music director for a performing arts company in my area, and I have been piano conductor for over a dozen musical plays such as *Oliver; Annie; Big River; Hello Dolly; Bye Bye Birdie; Peter Pan; You're a Good Man, Charlie Brown;* and *Beauty and the Beast.*

"I have provided the music for local beauty pageants, concerts in the park, and Fourth of July pageants. I have performed for many benefits to raise money for projects in our community and most recently played for a religious concert. I also have served as a judge for music talent in our area. Currently I teach thirty-two private piano students, and I am the church pianist/organist as well.

"I began working at Our Lady of Miracles Catholic School, a private Catholic school in Gustine, California, eight years ago, and I now work three days a week teaching music classes from kindergarten through eighth grade. This came about after the Assistant Superintendent of Schools saw me at work and hired me immediately to do music at her school. Most recently I was appointed to a visual and performing arts committee to integrate performing arts in the schools in our diocese.

"When designing music programs for children, my main concern is to teach a love for the art of music. I believe it is best done at the earliest age possible, for a love for music and performing arts will stay with children all their lives, as it did in mine. It is well known that bringing music and liberal arts to students is important on so many levels and ensures a broad and rich education. It reinforces social skills and positive attitudes and values and supports growth and intellectual enrichment. The value of the arts serves not only to develop personal intellectual growth, but also to sharpen judgment and interpersonal decision making. The key is to start with young children, and I know almost no other way to get and keep a small child's attention than with music.

"I truly love children and music. I have never been sorry I perform in public. I get so much enjoyment out of it. It is my life's work, just like numbers are the accountant's work and law is the lawyer's. To others I say, go for it if you feel it is in your heart!"

## Meet Mike Watson

Mike Watson, head of Watson Entertainment, Inc., is a recording artist at Uniworld Records in Atlanta, Georgia. He attended West Georgia College and majored in music.

"I started playing professionally in 1980 as lead guitarist and harmony singer for a band on the circuit," explains Watson. "I have been fascinated with music as long as I can remember, and I turned that dream into reality with a lot of hard work and perseverance and never settling for second best or taking 'no' for an answer.

"When I'm playing in town, a typical day is the following: I get up about noon and do everyday things like cutting the grass, etc. Then I work at the club from 9:00 P.M. until 1:00 or 2:00 A.M. Entertaining is what I do. Naturally, it is always a party atmosphere. When I go to different states doing shows, it's somewhat similar, except I get to see places and people in one day I probably would have never met and maybe not ever see again.

"I love almost every part of my job. I consider myself to be so fortunate because I am able to do the one thing I love doing most—earn a living at making music.

"My least favorite part is dealing with people who have had a little too much to drink, and every now and then having to deal with less than desirable booking agents who send you to a job that isn't quite what they painted it to be.

"My advice to others is if you have a genuine dream, never give up! If you know in your heart you have what it takes to succeed in your chosen profession, go for it!"

## Meet Rudy Gonzales

Rudy Gonzales is a "Cowboy Poet and Western Humorist" who travels all over the United States and Canada, performing his original and traditional cowboy poetry and songs at conventions, rodeos, fairs, banquets, and other gatherings. He is the founder and director of the Idaho State Cowboy Poetry Gathering, now in its eleventh year, and also publishes the *American Cowboy Poet Magazine.* Additionally he has written and produced two videos of his performances, "The Liar's Hour" and "Cowboy Poetry Live." Though he has shared his poetry and music with literally thousands of people, Rudy says that two of his most famous audience members were former president Gerald Ford and former vice-president Dan Quayle.

When he's not busy traveling and performing, Rudy "lives the cowboy life" with his wife Rose on their small ranch in Idaho. He grew up on a ranch in Colorado and now uses that lifelong experience to be a rancher, horse trainer instructor, and instructor of farrier science (horseshoer). "In one form or another, I have been doing what I do ever since I can remember," says Gonzales. "And it's what I want to do.

"I grew up in the cattle business. My father was a sought-after horse trainer and farrier. I spent over thirty years in the marketing field as the national sales manager for a Texas meat company. But none of the values of today's society appeal to me. I threw it all away to go back to a cowboy life. Then the entertainment business came calling on me. I have always enjoyed entertaining people and making them laugh.

"I have a home-office at my ranch in Idaho. The atmosphere is warm, but busy. Feeding livestock is the first order of my day, but then I turn my attention to the phone. Calls usually start very early. Negotiations for shows seem to occupy most of the day between calls and faxed agreements. Many performances come mid-week, and weekends generally find me out of town performing."

## Meet Chris Murphy

Chris Murphy is a professional musician, entertainer, record producer, and entertainment buyer as well as a part-time disc jockey at a college radio station. He began music lessons as a teenager and later attended Berkley College of Music in Boston. His father was also a musician, and Chris often played in bands with him before going on the road with his own band in 1978.

"I don't know how to do anything else," says Murphy. "Music is one of the few things I was good at and could take pride in. As a teenager, I felt that music stood out as something that was fun and that I excelled at. I started playing the saxophone at age seventeen and started playing in bands about the same time. I was in love with the blues long before I became a blues musician.

"My work atmosphere is great; I play in blues clubs four to six nights a week. I also spend at least an hour a day on the phone, organizing gigs and musicians. I meet a lot of interesting, talented, and funny people. I receive a lot of respect and love from the audiences I perform for. There is nothing that can replace the feeling of being on stage with a great band on a good night! I also have time to spend with my daughter in the daytime during the week, though occasionally I am away for the weekend.

"I enjoy the fact that when I go out to earn money, I am going out to play. How many people can say that?

"My advice is to never ever quit. The people who hang in there are the ones who inherit the entertainment business!"

### Meet Lionel Ward

Lionel Ward first became interested in being a musician when he was only nine years old and his mother bought him an Airline guitar for Christmas. Now he tours North America and Europe as the lead singer for the New World Band, a music group that entertains audiences with classic and contemporary rock and country songs.

Lionel was discovered by the late Wolfman Jack, who noticed Lionel's resemblance to Elvis Presley and invited him to a meeting. (Even now the band ends each performance with a tribute to Elvis.) Lionel's manager then sent a demo tape to Wolfman Jack's record label, Sonic Records, Inc., and the New World Band began recording under the Sonic label.

"I came from a musical family, so there was always music in the house," Ward says. "Music is therapy for the soul. It is the greatest feeling in the world to be able to play in front of an audience and see the enjoyment you give them. If you can relieve them of the everyday burdens of life for just a few minutes, you've done something important. The natural high you get from doing a live show cannot be compared to anything else. The only way you can achieve this feeling is through the music. And the beautiful thing is that it is all natural. Being able to sing and play an instrument is a God-given talent; you cannot buy this anywhere. You have to be born with it. It is a blessing to be able to share it with your audience.

"One thing I learned very early in the entertainment business is that every performance has to be the best you can possibly do. The key is to be able to sing your songs like they are being performed for the very first time. It may actually be the thousandth time you have sung that song, but in my opinion, it should be a thousand times better than the first. The people in the audience have chosen to take the time out of their evening to come and hear you play. You do not want to disappoint them, and I always make sure I do my very best whether there are five people in the audience or five thousand.

"My job as lead singer is to ensure that all arrangements have been made for the band. How big is the stage? How much room do I have to move around? The size of the show will tell us which public address system we are going to use for the evening. What lighting system is going to be used? How many people are we going to need for the road crew? I must ensure that all of this is taken care of, because it affects my show tremendously if I cannot hear the band or we can't see because someone forgot to put up a spotlight.

"As far as what work I actually do, I am involved with every aspect, right down to the last microphone sound check. You cannot measure how many hours are involved because some shows take days. If you count the actual rehearsal time, driving to the gigs, set up and tear down times, and sound checks, you would think we were insane. Our lives are devoted to music, but it is a labor of love. Sometimes we are gone from our homes for weeks. Living in hotels, doing radio and television interviews, is not one big party. I am very fortunate because for as long as I have been doing this, I have never considered it work. I truly love what I am doing.

"I love recording in the studio. It is like taking a piece of your life and freezing it in time. But I also love performing live. Again, there is no better feeling in the world than when the audience is wrapped up in your song and you are taking them on a journey. Sometimes I get so involved in the show that when I open my eyes, everyone is standing and cheering with tears in their eyes. It is then that I know they have felt the same things I have in the song.

"There is no downside in this business as far as I'm concerned. I am very fortunate that my wife travels with me and shares my dreams. For some people, I think a downside would be having to leave their family.

"My advice to others is to follow your dreams and what you feel in your heart. This business is very rough and unforgiving at times. But if you believe in yourself and you have the burning desire to make it, then you will. This business cannot be measured by hours or even days. It cannot be measured by money, either, though we need money to survive. If you truly believe in yourself and your music, everything else will fall into place.

"Many times you will hear me thank the audience for their support through the years. I was born a poor boy—rich with love and dreams, though—and I am definitely living my dreams!"

### Meet John A. Roberts

John A. Roberts attended Montgomery College, Rockville campus, majoring in speech and drama and then attended the University of Maryland at College Park majoring in radio and television.

In August of 1996, he competed in the National DJ of the Year competition in Atlantic City and was ranked in the top ten DJ's nationally. In January of 1997, he was awarded the Best Club DJ of 1996 in Las Vegas by the American DJ awards. He has spoken at numerous DJ conventions and expos nationally and in Canada and has written articles for magazines like *Mobile Beat, DJ Times,* and the *ADJA News.*

"I started as a stand up comic in the late 60's early to mid 70's," says Roberts. "I learned from the school of hard knocks as I was one of the first in this profession. While in the Air Force I competed in the AF talent show, Tops in Blue competition. I won first place in comedy and went on to worldwide competition.

"Currently I am owner of John Roberts' Roving Records, my personal DJ and karaoke service. I am also founder and national operations manager of the American Disc Jockey Association and owner of The DJ Training Center, the nation's first full-service independent training facility.

"I started DJing while still in the AF, at the USO club in Washington, DC in 1973. In 1975, when I was about to get out of the service, I had this totally unique idea. I would be like a band and play music at clubs, weddings, and parties, yet I would be a DJ and play records. I could go anywhere, be MOBILE! I had absolutely NO idea that someone else might have this idea, too. I certainly had never heard of it and knew of no one who did it. Many people close to me thought I was crazy and should pursue a real job. No one knew disco was brewing right around the corner! That's when DJs truly became accepted as a form of entertainment.

"I always wanted to get into broadcasting and wanted to keep up with my comedy. I figured this could be a stepping-stone in both directions. But after doing stand-up comedy and doing stage shows in high school and college, I loved the live audience.

"In radio you played to a wall. In a club or party, I was playing to live people and could feel the people and see their instant reaction to things I did. It was totally spontaneous. This is what attracted me to this particular format of entertainment. I could be self-employed and fulfill the American dream doing something I really loved. How many people can say that every time they work it's a party!

"But it's also a business and must be treated as such. There are legal ramifications in as much as we deal with contracts. There is a responsibility there. Music and supplies must be ordered and maintained. Keeping up with music is a major expense! These are the tools of the trade. Equipment must be purchased and maintained. There are promotions, marketing, advertising, hiring, firing, bookkeeping, and all the other normal procedures that any office or business encompasses.

"My days are busy. I am responsible for answering phones and handling customer inquiries, performing the negotiations and attending to contracts, training and scheduling DJs, ordering supplies and music, promoting the business, making advertising decisions, cataloging music, and creating and printing our karaoke catalogs.

"Then at night I will perform at a party. This requires more than just playing music. DJs work as coordinators between the host and guests. We take requests from party goers and, in general, try to keep everyone involved and happy.

"What I like most about this career is that I am my own boss. I can pick and choose the shows I do. I get to work in exciting places and meet exciting, sometimes famous, people. Being a mobile DJ has led to some interesting job opportunities for me. I did a television show like *American Bandstand* for over three years. I was a part of over thirty to forty radio and television commercials, performed on radio, was one of the original hosts of the *Home Shopper's Club of Virginia,* auditioned for a movie, and have been able to travel all over the United States.

"On the downside, there are no benefits that you ordinarily receive from an employer (unless you are willing to pay for them). It's very hard on my personal and social life. My average time to get to sleep is 3:00 to 4:00 A.M.

"My advice is that people should realize that this is a business and that it must be treated as such. I'd advise others to never burn bridges. Create friendly competitors and network, network, network. Learn to entertain, and to think on your feet. Even though we play CDs and other people's music, we still are entertainers. Always be willing to learn new tricks and techniques to stay on top. The minute you think you know it all is the minute your competition starts getting ahead of you."

### Meet Sean M. Meaney

Sean M. Meaney is owner of Sterling Entertainment of Tempe, Arizona.

"I started in the music business in 1984," says Meaney. "When I first started doing this, I couldn't believe that people would pay me to perform at parties. (Of course, I was only fifteen at the time.) A few years later I got my first chance to work in a nightclub. With people asking me to do private parties, it just took off. The hardest part was learning about equipment. I did not go to school for any technical training, so it was all done by trial and error.

"After fourteen years, my love for performing has evolved into a company that performs at weddings, bar/bas mitzvahs and corporate events. And I still learn new things every day.

"We are one of the few DJ/entertainment companies that do this full-time. During the week there is a lot of office work. That involves booking jobs, going to meet clients, and finding new ways to entertain people. A day starts off in the office, working on different marketing ideas. If there are no clients to see, I continue to pursue these efforts all day. On Friday we get ready for the weekend. That includes getting all of the equipment ready for the DJs. We want to make sure that everything is all set.

"Some seasons are busier than others. The wedding season is always a hectic one. Besides running the office, I still go out to do shows. All together I put in about sixty-plus hours per week.

"My favorite part of this job remains my love for entertaining. And I enjoy working for myself. On the down side, it is very difficult to find reliable people to hire to do shows. Also, running your own company is not easy.

"My advice to others is to set your goals and stick to that path. There are many areas in this business to go into—just pick one and proceed!"

### FOR MORE INFORMATION

There are literally hundreds of professional associations for musicians and dancers. Contact any of the following for more information about employment in this field.

American Choral Directors
    Association (ACDA)
  P.O. Box 6310
  Lawton, OK 73506

American Federation of Musicians
    (AFM)
  1501 Broadway, Suite 600
  New York, NY 10036

American Federation of Television
    and Radio Artists (AFTRA)
  260 Madison Avenue
  New York, NY 10016

American Guild of Music (AGM)
  5354 Washington Street
  Box 3
  Downers Grove, IL 60515

American Guild of Musical Artists
    (AGMA)
  1727 Broadway
  New York, NY 10019

American Guild of Organists (AGO)
  475 Riverside Drive, Suite 1260
  New York, NY 10115

American Federation of Musicians
  1501 Broadway, Suite 600
  New York, NY 10036

American Music Conference (AMC)
  5140 Avenida Encinas
  Carlsbad, CA 92008

American Musicological Society
  201 South Thirty-Fourth Street
  University of Pennsylvania
  Philadelphia, PA 19104

American Symphony Orchestra
    League (ASOL)
  777 Fourteenth Street, NW,
    Suite 500
  Washington, DC 20005

Academy of Country Music (ACM)
  500 Sunnyside Boulevard
  Woodbury, NY 11797

Association of Canadian Orchestras
  56 The Esplanade, Suite 311
  Toronto, Ontario
  Canada M5E IA7

Black Music Association (BMA)
  1775 Broadway
  New York, NY 10019

Broadcast Education Association
  National Association of
    Broadcasters
  1771 N Street, NW
  Washington, DC 20036

Broadcast Music, Inc. (BMI)
  320 West Fifty-Seventh Street
  New York, NY 10019

Chamber Music America
  545 Eighth Avenue
  New York, NY 10018

Chorus America
  Association of Professional Vocal
    Ensembles
  2111 Sansom Street
  Philadelphia, PA 19103

College Music Society
  202 West Spruce
  Missoula, MT 59802

Concert Artists Guild (CAG)
  850 Seventh Avenue, Room 1003
  New York, NY 10019

Country Music Association (CMA)
  P.O. Box 22299
  One Music Circle South
  Nashville, TN 37203

Gospel Music Association (GMA)
  P.O. Box 23201
  Nashville, TN 37202

International Conference of
    Symphony and Opera Musicians
    (ICSOM)
6607 Waterman
St. Louis, MO 63130

Metropolitan Opera Association
    (MOA)
Lincoln Center
New York, NY 10023

National Academy of Popular Music
    (NAPM)
885 Second Avenue
New York, NY 10017

National Academy of Recording Arts
    and Sciences (NARAS)
303 North Glen Oaks Boulevard,
    Suite 140
Burbank, CA 91502

National Association of Music
    Theaters
John F. Kennedy Center
Washington, DC 20566

National Association of Schools
    of Music
11250 Roger Bacon Drive, Suite 21
Reston, VA 22091

National Orchestral Association
    (NOA)
474 Riverside Drive, Room 455
New York, NY 10115

National Symphony Orchestra
    Association (NSOA)
JFK Center for the Performing Arts
Washington, DC 20566

Opera America
777 Fourteenth Street, NW,
    Suite 520
Washington, DC 20005

Radio-Television News Directors
    Association
1717 K Street, NW, Suite 615
Washington, DC 20006

Screen Actors Guild (SAG)
7065 Hollywood Boulevard
Hollywood, CA 90028

Society of Professional Audio
    Recording Studios
4300 Tenth Avenue North, #2
Lake Worth, FL 33461

Touring Entertainment Industry
    Association (TEIA)
1203 Lake Street
Fort Worth, TX 76102

Women in Music
P.O. Box 441
Radio City Station
New York, NY 10101

For information on purchasing directories about colleges and universities that teach dance, including details on the types of courses offered and scholarships, write to:

National Dance Association
1900 Association Drive
Reston, VA 22091
(800) 321-0789

A directory of dance, art and design, music, and theater programs may be purchased from:

National Association of Schools of
    Dance
    11250 Roger Bacon Drive, Suite 21
    Reston, VA 22090

For information on all aspects of dance, including job listings, send a self-addressed stamped envelope to:

American Dance Guild
    31 West Twenty-First Street,
        Third Floor
    New York, NY 10010

A directory of dance companies and related organizations, plus other information on professional dance, is available from:

Dance/USA
    777 Fourteenth Street, NW,
        Suite 540
    Washington, DC 20005

## CHAPTER 3

# CAREERS IN RADIO AND TELEVISION

A celebrity is a person who works hard all his life to become well known, and then wears dark glasses to avoid being recognized.

—Fred Allen

A variety of careers is available for those entertainment professionals who wish to focus on radio and television work. Actors, musicians, and dancers have already been covered in previous chapters. In this chapter we will focus on other types of television and radio entertainers and personalities.

## THE WORLD OF RADIO AND TELEVISION

Announcers and newscasters are well known to radio and television audiences. Radio announcers, often called disc jockeys, select and introduce recorded music; present news, sports, weather, and commercials; interview guests; and report on community activities and other matters of interest to their audience. If a written script is required, they may do the research and writing. They often ad-lib much of the commentary. They also may operate the control board, sell commercial time to advertisers, and write commercial and news copy.

Some announcers at large stations specialize in sports, weather, or general news and may be called newscasters or anchors. Others are news analysts. In smaller stations, one announcer may do everything.

News anchors, or a pair of co-anchors, present news stories and introduce in-depth videotaped news or live transmissions from on-the-scene reporters.

Broadcast news analysts, called commentators, present news stories and also interpret them and discuss how they may affect the nation or listeners.

Show hosts interview guests about their lives, work, or topics of current interest. Announcers frequently participate in community activities.

Radio and television announcers and newscasters number about fifty thousand. Nearly all are staff announcers, but some are freelance announcers who sell their services for individual assignments to networks and stations or to advertising agencies and other independent producers.

## ON THE JOB

Announcers and newscasters usually work in well-lighted, air-conditioned, soundproof studios. Since many radio and television stations are on the air twenty-four hours a day, the broadcast day is long. Announcers can expect to work unusual hours. Many present early morning shows, when large numbers of people are getting ready for work or already commuting. Other announcers may do late night newscasts.

Television and radio professionals work within tight schedule constraints, which can be physically and mentally stressful. Still, for many announcers, the intangible rewards, creative work, many personal contacts, and satisfaction of becoming widely known, far outweigh the disadvantages of irregular and often unpredictable hours, work pressures, and disrupted personal lives.

## TRAINING AND QUALIFICATIONS

High school courses in English, public speaking, drama, foreign languages, computers, and electronics are valuable, and hobbies such as sports and music are additional assets. Students may gain valuable experience at campus radio or television facilities and at commercial stations. Some stations and cable systems offer financial assistance and on-the-job training in the form of internships, apprentice programs, co-op work programs, scholarships, or fellowships.

Persons considering enrolling in a broadcasting school should contact personnel managers of radio and television stations as well as broadcasting trade organizations to determine the school's reputation for producing suitably trained candidates.

Announcers who operate transmitters must obtain a Federal Communications Commission (FCC) restricted radio-telephone operator permit.

Entry to this occupation is highly competitive. While formal training in broadcast journalism from a college or technical school (private broadcasting school) is valuable, station officials pay particular attention to taped auditions that show an applicant's delivery and television appearance and style on commercials, news, and interviews.

### Desirable Qualities

Announcers must have a pleasant and well-controlled voice, good timing, excellent pronunciation, and correct English usage. Television announcers need a neat, pleasing appearance as well. Knowledge of theater, sports, music, business, politics, and other subjects likely to be covered in broadcasts improves chances for success.

### BUILDING A CAREER

Those hired by television stations usually start out as production secretaries, production assistants, researchers, or reporters and are given a chance to move into announcing if they show an aptitude for on-air work. Newcomers to television broadcasting also may begin as news camera operators. A beginner's chance of landing an on-air newscasting job is remote, except possibly at a small radio station. In radio, newcomers generally start out taping interviews and operating equipment.

Announcers usually begin at a station in a small community and, if qualified, may move to a better paying job in a large city. Announcers also may advance by hosting a regular program as a disc jockey, sportscaster, or other specialist. In the national networks, competition for jobs is particularly intense, and employers look for college graduates with at least several years of successful announcing experience.

### JOB OUTLOOK

Competition for jobs as announcers will be very keen because the broadcasting field typically attracts many more job seekers than there are jobs. Small radio stations are more inclined to hire beginners, but the pay is low.

Because competition for ratings is so intense in major metropolitan areas, large stations will continue to seek announcers and newscasters who have proven that they can attract and retain a large audience. Newscasters who are knowledgeable in such areas as business, consumer, and health news may have an advantage over others. While specialization is more common at larger stations and the networks, many smaller stations also encourage it.

Little change in the employment of announcers is expected through the year 2005, due to the slowing in the growth of new radio and television stations and cable systems. Most openings in this relatively small field will arise from the need to replace those who transfer to other kinds of work or leave the labor force. Many announcers leave the field because they can't advance to better paying jobs. Employment in this occupation is not significantly affected by downturns in the economy. If recessions cause advertising revenues to fall, stations tend to cut behind-the-scenes workers rather than announcers and broadcasters.

## SALARIES

Salaries in broadcasting vary widely but, as a rule, they are higher in television than in radio, higher in larger markets than in small ones, and higher in commercial than in public broadcasting.

According to a survey conducted by the National Association of Broadcasters and the Broadcast Cable Financial Management Association, the average salary for radio news announcers is about $27,901. Salaries range from $23,000 in the smallest markets to $39,291 in the largest markets. Sports announcers' average is $38,950, ranging from $26,663 in the smallest markets to $75,029 in the largest.

Among television announcers, news anchors' average salary is $65,520, ranging from $24,935 in the smallest markets to $199,741 in the largest.

## PROFILES

### Meet Sylvia Perez

Sylvia Perez is a WLS-TV Channel 7 anchor in Chicago. She has worked in broadcasting since 1983.

"I attended journalism school at the University of Oklahoma and began my journalism career in 1983," says Perez. "My first job was in my hometown of Lawton, Oklahoma. I did morning news cut-ins and daily reporting. In 1984 I made the decision to move to another small station in

Amarillo, Texas, because the Lawton station did not have the live satellite units needed to provide live capabilities.

"What an exciting time of my life this turned out to be! I received a phone call from an agent who was familiar with my demo tape (a tape showing a sample of my work), who asked if I would like to be represented by that company. The company had already successfully forwarded the tape on to a station in Denver, Colorado, that was showing interest in me. With only six months experience in Amarillo, I moved to Denver to become a morning news anchor and weekday reporter. I had only worked in a small market and in a very short time, I was headed to an exciting city with a medium-sized market and a very professional newscast.

"After a two-year stint in Denver, I started to feel the hours take their toll. I had to arrive at 4:00 A.M. to write the news that I would present on the 6:00 A.M. show. That meant getting to bed really early so that I could get up at 2:30 A.M. and be at work on time. Needless to say, this was very difficult. In addition, I didn't see the possibility of upward movement. So I decided to move on.

"Incredibly, with no forewarning, I received a call from an NBC station. The voice on the other end of the phone said, 'I've seen your tape. Would you like to be a Houston weekend anchor?' He attempted to hire me over the phone, but I flew out for an interview and decided subsequently it would be a good career move. I spent the next two years in Houston as medical reporter and weekend anchor. After that, I decided that medical reporting was not for me and, with the aid of an agent, I received a number of job offers. Two of the offers were in Chicago. My ultimate choice was WLS-TV, where I was hired as a weekday reporter and weekend anchor. Happily, in September 1992, I became the co-anchor of Eyewitness News with Linda Yu (at 11:30 A.M.), the first newscast in Chicago anchored by two women.

"Being an anchor is really not the glamorous job everyone seems to think it is. That's because sitting behind the studio anchor desk is only a very small portion of the whole job. A typical day means rush, rush, rush. Since I don't get off the air until noon, I get a late start on whatever my assigned story is. It may be a story that a reporter from another station is covering and might have started much earlier. That means that I have to play catch-up from the start and work fast. I may only have a short time to put the story together, but I still must be thorough and make sure that I don't omit any important details. Of course, if there's some important late-breaking news, I'll be assigned to that story, which may mean going out on the street, doing interviews, gathering all the facts, and then writing the story. The story is either presented live or as a self-contained piece for one of the newscasts, usually in the 5:00 or 6:00 P.M. news spot.

"The reality of the job is that stations look for aggressive reporters who are not afraid to work hard. The career is demanding and extremely competitive. If you are not committed, you'll never make it. And you always have to be available, twenty-four hours a day, seven days a week. You must be eager to learn, since every day you are put in new situations that you must translate efficiently to the viewer. Sometimes you have to go on air live the minute you reach the scene of a newsworthy event, so you must really be able to think on your feet quickly.

"You need to be able to conduct effective interviews with people in all walks of life, and you must have the background and knowledge to put the story together into a cohesive and interesting form. You have to be able to deal with death and destruction, which all too often are central to the news story, while still maintaining your professionalism and asking the important questions with compassion and accuracy.

"Stations no longer want personalities who simply read the news. You must be able to go out on the street, get your hands dirty, and work, work, work! In this profession, you have to be flexible and ready to handle almost anything.

### Meet Carol Stein

Carol Stein's one-hour program on WEAT radio in Florida is called *Business Opportunities with Carol Stein.*

"My background is a bit unusual in that I did not major in communications," says Stein. "As an undergraduate I went to the Wharton Business School, where I majored in finance and electrical engineering. Then I went on to obtain my M.B.A at Wharton.

"Entering the world of business, I traveled all over the globe as a consultant for several Fortune 500 companies in a number of diverse fields. At the other end of the spectrum, I also had experience in cheerleading, modeling, aerobics, teaching, and acting. My mother is a public relations specialist and my father has a Ph.D. in chemical engineering and owns his own business, so I guess I'm a product of both worlds.

"When you have experience, you make contacts and projects come to you. But when you are first starting out, you have two options. You can either try to get hired at a television or radio station or you can approach a station with an idea for a show you wish to produce. At the beginning of my media career, when I was living in Washington, DC, I produced and hosted a television show. This allowed me to learn every aspect of television and also gave me the opportunity to interview many high-level personalities, including President Clinton. When I moved to Florida, I took my television concept and adapted it to radio. Though I had a lack of media experience at the time, I felt confident to handle all aspects of the project. My preference was to approach it that way, so that I could become familiar with all aspects of this business—producing, being on the air, hiring talented individuals, marketing, selling, editing, and everything else. As a result, I know how to work the camera, do audio, and set up lighting. I write scripts. I know how to do graphics. I can work in front of a computer performing all the digital animation.

"Every Saturday, I feature three business entrepreneurs, producers, entertainers, or marketing or public relations specialists from all over the world. I find out how they got started, what problems they've faced, what advice they would offer, and how success has changed their lives. My experience is that these people are kind, down-to-earth individuals who have worked hard to earn the respect of others.

"Many people want to get into the field, but most are not aware of 99 percent of the effort I expend behind the scenes. Most are intrigued by my career and often say, 'Oh, you're so lucky; you meet people like Dave Thomas (founder of Wendys), you're invited to lots of great parties, your life is so exciting.' But they don't realize that part of the reason for going to functions and parties is to promote both the show and myself and to meet new people who would be interesting to have as guests. (I've never had anyone turn me down.) Unfortunately, this makes my work week a seven-day experience. I always have to go, even if I'm tired. But since I love my career, I feel as if I'm not really working.

"I am involved in all aspects of the show: getting the sponsors, booking the guests, doing the research, creating interview questions, performing the interviews, and editing tapes. So for every hour that I'm on the air, there are twenty to forty hours of preparation time that no one sees (and this is what makes the show so good). I study financial reports, perform research at the library, visit pertinent sites, read company literature, do anything I can to familiarize myself with the prospective guest. It is my goal to get to know my interview subjects well. Then I create new and different questions for each interview. As a result, I am often up until 2:00 A.M.

staring at my computer, thinking I still have hours of work to complete my task. But I feel it's worth it because I can guarantee my guests that they will have a good time and be asked solid business questions.

"In this business you've got to be confident about your abilities and able to take rejection. Since the commodity you are putting out there is you, it's hard not to take it personally when you are criticized because it feels personal. But you have to believe in yourself and what you do so passionately that you are willing to keep trying and to endure—no matter what. You must be willing to commit to the time and effort and be patient until you are able to realize your dream.

"You also must be prepared to do whatever is necessary to achieve success. For instance, my job requires that I do a lot of selling; whether it's calling up to secure a guest for a show, talking to sponsors, or promoting a newspaper article about me or the show.

"It's important to remember that as a talk show host, the people you are interviewing are the stars, so it is your responsibility to get them comfortable enough so they can shine. Within them are the stories that people want to hear, so you need to keep your ego in check. If you are truly a good person who cares about others, people will trust you and feel comfortable with you. And if you're ethical and honest, you'll establish the right kind of reputation, which will stay with you throughout your career.

"One of the best parts of this career is that I'm excited by my work every day. I'm never bored. I meet many interesting, wonderful people, some of whom have become my friends. They encourage me and continually expand my sphere of knowledge. It's like getting my M.B.A every day."

## Meet Brian R. Powell

Brian R. Powell has been a radio personality and DJ on WCIL-FM radio in Carbondale, Illinois, for the past two years. His show is featured from 3:00 in the afternoon until 7:00 P.M.

"As a sophomore in high school, I was actually flunking English," Powell says. "My teacher took me aside and said, 'You know Brian, you are articulate and have a nice voice. You should try out for the high school radio station.' I had no idea that such a thing existed, but I decided to check into it. Before I knew it, I had completed an audition and was doing a five-minute sportscast every day. Joyfully, it soon dawned on me that I could pursue this as a career, though I didn't know how to go about it at that point.

"I worked in high school radio for three years and gained a substantial amount of experience in proper breathing techniques, how to present myself, technical aspects of the business, and other performance and behind-the-scenes endeavors, such as writing and editing.

"When I was a senior in high school I had an electronics teacher who was also chief engineer for WBBX, a suburban radio station in Highland Park, Illinois. He was able to get me a part-time job at the station for a whopping $2.30 an hour. After a stint in radio sales, I enrolled at Southern Illinois University, where I secured a job at SIU's radio station, WSRJ. The classes that I took in radio and television were helpful, but my hours at the radio station provided a wealth of information. I settled in to enjoy my radio years there.

"Following this, I got a part-time position at WHBI in Heron, where I worked my way up to the prestigious morning position. While there, I increased my knowledge further and gained experience in doing play-by-play (the most difficult job in broadcasting). After about three years, I secured the morning position at WTAO in Murphysboro, just 10 miles away.

"Circumstances pushed me out of the radio business for a few years, until I moved back to Carbondale in 1992 and found my way to WCIL-FM. When I first came to the station, I was assigned the overnight shift from 2:00 A.M. until 6:00 A.M. Then I volunteered to take the 10:00 A.M. to 2:00 P.M. slot for a vacationing DJ, and for a while I did both shifts. As a result, I impressed the general manager and won the afternoon spot. I'm happy with this time slot, because I get to sleep as late as I wish whereas morning DJs must wake up at 4:30 or 5:00 A.M. Another bonus of this job is that I don't have to get dressed up; I frequently arrive at the station in sweatpants and a T-shirt and open-toed sandals. Most of the time I'm not seen by anybody, unless we have a radio tour on the calendar.

"I enjoy meeting the touring elementary and high school students. Often they have a preconceived notion of how complicated a radio station must be, and I have the opportunity to teach them about how simple it all is. The one negative aspect to these occasions is that I don't get to enjoy the privacy I usually have. When I'm alone in the radio room, I feel I have the freedom to take chances, let my mind go, and be creative with no one staring at me. I want to be known, but not well known. Television is a totally different medium. Those involved in television understand that since their physical image is commonplace, they can't go out in public without being recognized and possibly approached. In radio my friends know who I am, but I don't have any pretenses about being famous.

"My ultimate goal is to do radio in Chicago, although I'd consider Milwaukee or St. Louis. The longer I am involved in radio, the more I realize I still have a way to go in perfecting my craft. But I'm very willing to put in the time and energy to accomplish this because I really enjoy what I'm doing.

"For me this job is really quite informal and simple. I come in about an hour early and read as much of the newspapers as possible: the *Chicago Tribune,* the *St. Louis Post Dispatch, Southern Illinois,* and a couple of other smaller local papers. I look through them to familiarize myself with what is newsworthy locally, regionally, and nationally. This is important because I frequently receive phone calls when we're on the air from people wanting information about things that are going on in the world.

"We also receive trade publications published by record companies, which provide a wealth of information about music and the bands that we're playing. So I'll look through those as well.

"When it's actually time to go on the air, I go into the studio to select the music to play. Since we're a top-forty station, most of the music that we present repeats itself regularly about every four or five hours. The newest music is played most often. But since I'm also able to play selections of my own from the music that's provided in the library, I'll browse through there looking for songs I haven't played recently or something that looks interesting. Once I've made my selections, I organize the order of the songs so that the music is presented in a pleasing sequence and avoids abrupt changes.

"Usually the DJ who's on before me will pull the commercials that I need for the first hour of the show. So when I arrive each day, there is a stack of those on the cart ready for me. Most of the commercials are prerecorded; but I do have some live reads. These are fun because I can really ham it up. And I have responsibility for organizing the commercials into what we call 'top sets' or groupings, to make sure competitors are not played back to back (for instance, playing an ad for Coca Cola and then one for Pepsi).

"On occasion I conduct brief interviews. I'm always free to proceed with such projects if I feel they would make good radio. For instance, we recently had an interesting situation involving George Harrison's sister, who used to live in a house in southern Illinois. Back in 1963, before the Beatles ever came to America, George Harrison visited and stayed with her in that home. Not only that, he played a few songs on guitar in one of the local restaurants in town. Subsequently, this house was sold to the Illinois Department of Mines and Minerals who wanted to tear it down. This became a controversy, with people taking one side or the other. Since there was considerable local interest in this issue, I did a number of live interviews with some of the people involved, including Louise Harrison herself. In the end, the house was preserved.

"Much of what comes out of my mouth is not pre-scripted. What I say is whatever feels right to say at the time. In general I try to minimize my speaking and emphasize the music, since I feel most people are listening at work or in their cars and have a desire to hear music, not talking.

"If you are interested in a career in radio, the first thing you should do is make the radio a priority. Listen to the DJs, what they say, and how they say it. Also be aware of what they don't say. When I was first starting out, I would try to repeat exactly what the DJ was saying right after it came out of his mouth, using the very same pacing and inflection. Try doing this— or any kind of performing for that matter—in front of an audience.

"In terms of classes, focus on English. It worked for me. I had B+s by the time I graduated. Also concentrate on journalism, psychology, and my personal favorite—political science. They complement radio work by sharpening your mind, thus allowing you to process information and think more quickly on your feet. These qualities are vital to success in radio.

"Perhaps the most important advice I could offer is to be prepared for failure because if you are prepared for that, you will definitely be prepared for success."

### Meet Chuck Woodford

Chuck Woodford is the morning show host on KXPK (The Peak) radio in Denver. He received a Bachelor of Arts degree in broadcast journalism from West Virginia University, working in the college radio station for three years in various capacities including production director and operations manager. He heartily recommends the college radio environment, which he believes taught him volumes.

"While I was growing up, my mom got me hooked on old-time radio shows like *The Shadow* and *X-1*," Woodford says. "When I got to college, I met several folks who shared the same passion that I had for the medium. As I've gotten older, I've become much more educated to the ways of the business side of the industry, but I still have a great passion for the 'theatre of the mind' aspect of the job.

"Doing a show in the morning is a completely different thing than doing it just about any other time of the day. People rely on you to be a news provider, a sportscaster, a competent weatherman, a traffic reporter, and an entertainer. You need to be up on current events and have a passion for what you do.

"The show runs from 5:30 A.M. until 10:00 A.M., so my day begins at about 4:30 A.M. when I get into work. I'm lucky in that I have a morning show producer who gets in before I do and spends about thirty minutes on the Internet, hunting down entertainment news. After I get there, we have a fifteen-minute meeting about what the focus of the show should be: Did anything interesting happen overnight? Do we have something cool to give away? Are there any shows we should be talking about (both upcoming concerts and TV shows from last night)?, etc. Once the show is over, we sit down with our program director and figure out what's up for the next day's show. I'm usually out of the building by 1:00 P.M., but then it's off to do a promotion or to go host a pre-show party before a big concert.

"One thing that surprised me about the morning slot is the amount of preparation that goes into the show. It's very time consuming, but when you're able to pull off a great bit the next day, you know that it was all worth it.

"What I like most about my job is that it's a great avenue for my personality. I get to be myself on the radio, and I have the freedom to pursue my own ideas about what the show should be. I also get to use the creativity of a very talented staff around me. Plus, I don't have to wear any shoes while I'm at work, which is nice!

"I would advise those just starting out to be prepared to work as hard as you can possibly imagine. Don't expect things to fall into your lap. Don't feel like you can get a really sweet gig and then coast right through it. There will always be somebody behind you willing to do the exact same job that you're doing, only with more energy and more excitement. So always push yourself."

## Meet Robin Truesdale

Robin Truesdale earned a Bachelor of Science degree in journalism from the University of Colorado, with an emphasis in broadcast management. She worked at Denver television station, KUSA-TV, for ten years as a videotape editor, and she has also done freelance work for FOX News in Denver and WXIA-TV in Atlanta. Throughout her career, she has attended many seminars and classes specific to video editing techniques and new technology.

"I was attracted to editing after watching my dad work in the advertising field," Truesdale says. "He was a producer and director when I was a child, and I sometimes went with him on shoots and edit sessions and got to watch him and the editor create advertising spots. It was fascinating to me to watch the editor sit at an enormous board full of buttons and switches and make magic happen on video, combining music, pictures, and effects. I loved the creativity involved and the respect that the editors had. My dad had favorites to work with, whom he felt were the most talented in the Atlanta area. I saw those top-notch video editors as being in the same league with film editors. Some had national reputations. And when I would see a national advertising spot that my dad had produced, I had a sense of pride. I guess I wanted to feel that pride for myself as an editor.

"My internship at KUSA in my senior year of college was definitely vital in my getting a job upon graduation. I was familiar with that specific newsroom and their expectations for news editors. It also allowed me to demonstrate my abilities to the staff. Experience is really the only way to learn how to edit. The internship, combined with my experiences with my father, helped me to understand the basic concepts of editing, and that understanding made me a good candidate when a job opening became available.

"The typical day for a television news editor involves a lot of downtime and then sudden bursts of activity. There are relaxed hours in the day when editors are waiting for scripts to be written, video to be shot, etc. Paperwork is done during this time, dubs are made, people joke around a lot, and the mood is very light. As news time gets closer, though, the mood becomes more serious, often intense, and everyone switches gears. Editors are expected to do their jobs in a short amount of time, and there is a lot of deadline pressure. As soon as scripts start coming in, work must be done very quickly, but also correctly and with style. Crews often feed video from the field, and it is the editor who receives this video and turns it around, sometimes within a matter of seconds, to get it on the air. The image of people running down halls with videotape in hand is very accurate. We occasionally have crashes in the hallway when people are rushing around during a newscast. So that element of the job is stressful and high pressure. It also can be exhilarating, and that is, in fact, what some people like most about the job. There is a terrific sense of satisfaction after a show is over and all has gone well.

"On the other hand, there is a lot of reprimanding when an element of the show crashes and burns. People have to take responsibility for their jobs because the results of their work are broadcast to thousands or millions of people. The consequences of doing a poor job are pretty severe.

"Editors in news generally work a forty-hour shift, with overtime a necessity during breaking news. An editor is generally on call at all times if something big happens, like an airplane crash or a large-scale emergency. You're expected to care enough about the station you work for to be there in a crisis situation, even if you are not called in right away. It's really just part of the job.

"I love the camaraderie of the news business. The atmosphere of delivering news, both good and bad, is probably somewhat like working in an emergency room. There are tragic moments, and there are triumphant ones, too. It creates a strong bond among employees…almost a family atmosphere. That is the part I like the most, the closeness among us all.

"On a personal level, there is a great sense of satisfaction of having done a job well. There are times when the editor is allowed a great deal of creativity, cutting feature stories for instance, and that is when I have the most fun as an editor. Some pieces can really impact viewers; that makes me feel good and also important. Taking elements of a story—pictures, interviews, sound, and sometimes music—and blending them all together to tell a story is a very personal thing. It requires skill and talent, and with editing you are rewarded every day by your own creations.

"The worst part of editing news is the tragic stories you come face to face with daily. You're exposed to the worst side of humanity, the most tragic and sad events regularly. I've edited many stories with tears streaming down my face. Those are the hard times, the ones that really challenge you as a human being. At those times, I wish I was in commercial production or some other aspect of editing, where you have more control over your material. But, of course, there are enough positives to balance it out.

"My advice to those interested in editing of any kind is to get internships! Get as many as you can while in school, even if they're not exactly the field you're interested in. Any experience in television or film, even in still photography or writing, will enhance your education and perhaps even change your mind about what you want to do. Hands-on experience is necessary.

"Also, be humble. Listen to others with experience in the field. Never think you know it all, because surely you don't. Every person you meet, every experience you have, even the negative ones, will teach you something, so you must be open to learning.

"Editing is a creative, artistic field. It is also technical, becoming digital, and computer based. Learning to operate equipment is critical, but a student of editing needs to do more than simply push buttons and put pictures together. It's a career that combines photography, technical skill, quick judgment, and artistic vision.

"Most of all, I would stress to others that you must have confidence in yourself and you should never give up. You can accomplish anything if you want it badly enough."

## Meet Judlyne A. Lilly

Judlyne A. Lilly earned a Bachelor of Science degree from Indiana State University, Terre Haute. She majored in theater and minored in radio and television. Lilly also earned a Master of Fine Arts degree in playwriting from the Catholic University of America, in Washington DC.

"I knew that I wanted a career in broadcasting at the age of ten or eleven when I saw Nancy Dickerson doing a five-minute news update on television," says Lilly. "From then on, I worked toward that goal. The Texas Association of Broadcasting in Houston awarded me (and two others) the opportunity to go to a summer workshop on broadcasting, and I stayed in touch with the host station, Channel 11, throughout my college years. As a result, I ended up with a reporting job when I graduated.

"I moved into radio about ten years ago because, quite frankly, I simply like it better. Today I am a radio news anchor at WTOP radio in Washington, DC.

"The profession of broadcasting contains all the things I like in my life: informing people, witnessing history, glamour (yes, even in radio), and that little ego boost when someone tells you that they heard about a major event from you.

"The anchors at WTOP are also writers. In fact, in many cases, we write our own copy. We also run our own boards, that is to say we are responsible for punching all the right buttons to get our microphones on and the correct reporter tapes (carts) on at the right time. And, of course, the same holds true for those all-important commercials.

"A typical day is generally very busy. Each day we come in and write our hour-long newscast. This means that we must be up on the day's events. Then we go in with a co-anchor in the studio and read the news, introduce weather and traffic every ten minutes, read the log—that's a rundown of what commercials go where, how much time for each section of the news, etc.—and generally try to sound like it's all very normal and natural.

"This position translates into an eight-hour day, without a lunch hour (we usually eat at our desks). Once the anchor shift is over, which can vary from day to day, if we're still on the clock, we work on news stories for the next day or for future airings.

"Our work atmosphere is one of hard work mixed with a little fun. The people at WTOP are very intelligent and mostly very funny.

"As far as I can see, there is no downside to this job, that is, unless you're one of those strange people who believes that being at work at 4:00 A.M. is a downside. The upside is the absolute pleasure of working in the field you love with people who feel the same way.

"When I speak to college groups or others interested in the business, I tell them that success in this business requires commitment (doesn't everything?). Also, I tell them that it's important to get a job before they graduate, even if it's an internship or part-time gofer position. There's nothing like already having your foot in the door before you graduate from college. The contacts you make are invaluable and will last the rest of your professional life."

## FOR MORE INFORMATION

For a list of schools that offer programs and courses in broadcasting, contact:

Broadcast Education Association
    1771 N Street NW
    Washington, DC 20036

For information on FCC licenses, write to:

Federal Communications Commission
    Consumer Assistance Office
    1270 Fairfield Road
    Gettysburg, PA 17325–7245
    (800) 322-1117

General information on the broadcasting industry is available from:

National Association of Broadcasters
    1771 N Street NW
    Washington, DC 20036

For information on careers in broadcast news, contact:

Radio-Television News Directors Association
    1717 K Street NW, Suite 615
    Washington, DC 20006

## CHAPTER 4

# CAREERS BEHIND THE SCENES

In the theater the audience wants to be surprised—but by things that they expect.

—Tristan Bernard, Contes, repliques et bon mots

Most people don't have any idea what goes on behind the scenes. They are unaware of how many professionals perform a variety of tasks in order to make a performance entertaining and successful.

Team spirit is of the utmost importance for the professionals who work together behind the scenes to create performances everyone can be proud of.

## JOBS BEHIND THE SCENES IN MUSIC

Those who work behind the scenes include stage managers, sound technicians, boom operators, sound/production mixers, music video producers, record producers, recording engineers, recordists, and re-recording mixers.

### Stage Managers

Stage managers are in charge of everything involved in onstage performances whether they are held at clubs, concert halls, state fairs, theaters, or any other arena. All aspects of a performance come under the stage manager's domain—curtain changes, lighting, sound—anything and everything that could have an effect upon the success of the performance. He or she is thus in charge of all technicians, assistants, and helpers—the entire staff.

Sometimes important stars travel with their own lighting and sound technicians crews. As a result, the stars feel they can relax in the fact that their crews are very familiar with what needs to be done and there are no unpleasant surprises before, during, or after performances.

### Sound Technicians/Sound Engineers

Sound technicians are important members of the behind-the-scenes staff. They answer to the tour coordinator and usually arrive at the location of the performance in advance of the performers. Along with the rest of the crew, sound technicians unload and set up the equipment and the instruments. All of the equipment must be positioned so that the instruments will sound best and vocals, if part of the performance, will blend in a pleasing manner.

Once things are set up, the vocalists and musicians arrive and the sound technicians prepare for a very important event—the sound check. This is accomplished by having each person play his or her instrument or sing, while technicians judge whether or not the sound is coming through properly. Obviously, any changes that need to be made will be taken care of before the show begins.

While the show is in progress, sound technicians are in charge of the soundboard, usually situated in front of the stage. In this position, they can adjust the volumes of voices and instruments.

After the show, sound technicians usually pack up the sound equipment. In some cases they may be responsible for checking all of the equipment to see what is not working properly or is in need of repair. Sometimes sound technicians are capable of actually taking care of the problem.

### Boom Operators

The boom is a large overhead microphone that hangs over the set. These technicians make sure that the boom is properly following the performers.

### Sound/Production Mixers

Sound/production mixers are in charge of the overall sound quality and the volume of the sound. Required when there is more than one microphone on the set, sound/production mixers make sure that sound is picked up and blended in a harmonious way.

## Music Video Producers

Music video producers are in charge of everything relating to the making of music videos. This includes all of the visual effects and interpretations of the songs vocal artists are endeavoring to promote. Producers oversee the entire production team including film editor, choreographer, photography director, and the rest of the team.

Music video producers must be superb problem solvers, have good visual and listening proficiencies, have the ability to work well with others, posess a good business sense, understand the business, and have good contacts in the industry.

## Record Producers

There are many people who are part of the process of record production. Perhaps most important is the record producer. Record producers have the responsibilities of handling all payroll tasks, supervising the recording sessions, helping to decide what songs will be recorded, and actually producing the records for the artists. Other responsibilities include finding a suitable recording studio, arranging the recording time, choosing an engineer, picking an arranger, and getting in touch with someone who can find the background musicians and vocalists needed. Record producers also will act as the heads of the operations, making sure everyone meets their responsibilities. During recording, the producer works hand-in-hand with the engineer to create the exact sound desired.

## Recording Engineers

Recording engineers operate the soundboard and other electrical equipment when recordings are made.

## Recordists

These technicians operate the tape machine and make sure that everything is recorded properly.

## Re-recording Mixers

Re-recording mixers complete soundtracks by adding background music, additional dialogue, or sound effects.

Behind-the-scenes technicians may find employment with a local or well-known regional band. The best strategy is to start small and try to work your way to larger and more well-known bands. Major tours usually traverse Los Angeles, New York City, and Nashville, although they may be found in almost any substantially sized city in the United States.

## JOBS BEHIND THE SCENES IN ACTING

Those who work behind the scenes in acting include stage directors, stage managers, technical directors, set designers, costume designers, hair stylists, makeup artists, lighting designers, sound designers, property designers, carpenters, scenic artists, special effects specialists, electricians, riggers, broadcast technicians, and wardrobe supervisors.

### Stage Directors

At the top of the stage hierarchy are stage directors who read each play to decide whether they are interested in directing it. If they decide to take on the project, they are in charge of coordinating the entire production of the play. Meetings then take place between director and playwright to decide about the best way to present it. Additional conversations will take place with the producer about issues including casting, budgets, production schedules, designers, and other details.

Directors are the ones who interpret the plays or scripts as they see fit. In addition, they may audition and select cast members, conduct rehearsals, and direct the work of the cast and crew. Directors use their knowledge of acting, voice, and movement to achieve the best possible performance and usually approve the scenery, costumes, choreography, and music.

Once directors have become familiar enough with the play to determine the approach and perspective they wish to take, they meet with designers to begin the process of creating costumes, scenery, sound effects, and lighting. With the aid of a stage manager, directors make hundreds of decisions in order to best represent the piece.

Once rehearsals begin, directors are the ones who instruct the cast about where they are to be positioned on stage, how they are to move, and what feelings and actions they should display. In the process, they rehearse the performers as they practice their lines and make suggestions for changes whenever they see fit.

Upon presentation, directors often like to attend a dress rehearsal or preview and position themselves in different parts of the theater in order to observe the reactions of people in the audience. Even at that point, changes may be made—if the director believes it can improve the play.

Directors and producers often work under stress as they try to meet schedules, stay within budgets, and resolve personnel problems while putting together a production.

## Stage Managers

Once the director leaves the production, stage managers have the final say on most everything to do with the play and its production. They are the ones who call the casts together to begin rehearsals. They see to it that everyone who is required is present. They send an assistant to inform the stars when they will be needed and when to be ready to go on stage. If necessary, they make arrangements for stand-ins. They are the ones who give the signal for the house lights to dim, signaling the fact that the production is about to begin.

Stage managers maintain a master script or a book containing all details of the play. Listed inside are the actors movements, entrance and exit cues, costume details, and lighting and sound cues. Any changes are recorded in the master book. They also maintain personal records on all cast members and backstage workers including names, addresses, and phone numbers.

Stage managers often have assistants who help with the backstage duties. If so, they are able to be out front to watch the play. In this way, they can stay attuned to changes or improvements that can be made.

## Technical Directors

Technical directors are assigned the task of coordinating all of the work of designers and their entire crews. They are responsible for making sure that all of the preliminary work moves forward on schedule and that everything fits together properly. They meet with lighting, property, and sound designers to work out details. Also, they make sure set changes and storage details work as planned. When on tour, technical directors aid other workers to make adjustments to fit the space and layouts of different theaters.

## Set Designers

Set designers are entrusted with the responsibility of the physical environment of the play. In order to successfully accomplish this, they research the time and place of the play. Uncovering typical architecture for the time and place, they make sketches and models of possible sets and present them to the director for his or her approval. Then they make detailed drawings and models (exactly to scale) using cardboard, wood, plastic, clay or other materials. The plans must show ways to prepare and move the pieces quickly and safely and how remaining sets may be stored offstage while one is being used onstage.

Set designers may meet with directors concerning details of construction costs and other relevant ideas. On the other hand, they may take their plans to two or three shops for bids. The designers then oversee the building and painting of the sets, whether this means creating stairs, mountains, balconies, or whatever is needed for the play.

## Costume Designers

Costume designers also must do some researching about the locale, period, and social background of the play. Libraries and museums are appropriate places to study clothing, styles, and fabrication. Once this phase is completed, they begin to draw sketches of costumes that will eventually need director approval. Once given, they bring the sketches to the theater costume shop to plan how to make them. If the production is taking place in a large city such as New York, costume designers may secure bids from two or three costume shops. They select the fabric, approve the clothing patterns, and oversee their progress as they are developed.

For plays that will take place with a modern setting, costume designers might shop for ready-made garments. Other pieces such as wigs or beards may be needed, and the costume designer will select them from a wig shop.

Once everything is secured, fittings are scheduled for cast members to check that the costumes are right. To make sure everything looks the way it should, a dress parade is held onstage under lights with scenery and props in place.

## Hairstylists and Makeup Artists

Hairstylists and makeup artists use cosmetics, pencils, greasepaints, brushes, and other materials to make the actors and actresses look like the characters they play. Makeup also may include hair, clay, or plastics to create wrinkles, warts, bald heads, teeth changes, burns, or scars. Even the actors' hands must be right for the characters they are playing.

## Lighting Designers

Lighting designers use lighting fixtures, patterns, color filters, and dimmers in order to create lighting effects. Referring to floor plans of the sets, they decide where to place each piece of equipment. The master electrician and lighting director plan the electric circuits for the equipment. The lighting board operator controls the lights in the theater throughout the play. Cue sheets tell the operator exactly when to turn each unit on and off. In some cases, a computer in the light board handles these details, which expands the effects of lighting designs. In order to make sure that circuits and lights are in proper working order, lighting designers report for work one hour early.

## Sound Designers

Sound designers are the individuals who create and direct the making of sound effects: drumbeats, sirens, breaking glass, whirling tornadoes. The designers are faced with choosing and directing placement of amplifiers, speakers, synthesizers, microphones, and other equipment. Once satisfied with the results, cue sheets are made up for the soundboard operator to follow during all performances. One or more sound technicians work during a show. One may work from a place in the audience mixing or blending the sounds the audience hears. Another, backstage, may control sounds the performers and musicians hear. A third worker may be in charge of handling prerecorded sounds or special sound effects. All wear intercom headsets to monitor the work going on at the time.

## Property Designers

Property designers are involved in planning and, in some cases, directing the making of pieces needed for productions—anything from palm trees to antique sofas. Other items they may be asked to provide are books, violins, spears, shields, or a wide variety of other items. They also may be asked to construct masks or hands for characters appearing as dragons, monkeys, monsters, donkeys, or any number of other animals.

## Carpenters and Scenic Artists

Working with materials like wood, canvas, muslin, metal, clay and other materials, carpenters and scenic artists are hired to build the sets and properties for a theatrical production.

## Special Effects Specialists

Special effects specialists are the ones who create, plan, and install the devices needed to make smoke, rain, snow, fog, or the like.

## Electricians

Electricians connect and mark the circuits for both sound and lighting effects.

## Riggers

Riggers do their work considerably above ground level; they hang lighting, sound equipment, and scenery from wires and ropes. They also are involved in working with pulleys and counterbalances to control the movable parts of any sets.

## Broadcast Technicians

Broadcast technicians operate and maintain the equipment used to record and transmit radio and television programs. They work with sound and video recorders, television cameras, transmitters, microphones, and equipment used for special effects.

## Wardrobe Supervisors

Once the play opens, wardrobe supervisors are in charge of all of the costumes. Crews are hired to keep shoes polished, suits brushed, broken zippers replaced, hems stitched. Costumes also may need to be adjusted to fit stand-ins. When on tour, the wardrobe supervisors and their helpers are charged with packing and unpacking the costumes and putting them in the dressing rooms.

All of the same opportunities open to actors and actresses are also available to those who work behind the scenes. This would include Broadway productions, regional plays, children's theater, summer stock, radio, television, and commercials.

## TRAINING FOR CAREERS BEHIND THE SCENES IN MUSIC

Though a formal education is not required for those who work behind the scenes in music, it can provide you with a concrete background of information and contacts. Many who are interested in this field acquire basic knowledge and experience by shadowing other individuals who are performing this kind of work.

Working as a volunteer in a community, church, or school production offers valuable experience that will help to elevate your marketability in the music business.

It's important for behind-the-scenes personnel to be able to work well with all kinds of people because they serve as a link in the chain that provides the totality of music performances. Other desirable characteristics include reliability; responsibility; a good ear for music; sufficient expertise in the areas of musical and technical knowledge; proficiency with the soundboard, sound equipment, and electronics; and a love of music.

## TRAINING FOR CAREERS BEHIND THE SCENES IN ACTING

At the high school level and sometimes the middle school level, many schools have programs in fine arts. Students who plan to work in theater should take part in school plays and musical shows. In high school they should take history, literature, art, and English.

Hopefuls for careers behind the scenes should get as much experience as possible working on productions at school, at church, or at a local theater. An association with a professional company is an added bonus. Working as a volunteer is a good idea. Part-time possibilities include local theater, dinner theater, and special events like benefits or rock concerts.

Candidates for these careers should plan on earning at least a bachelor's degree in fine arts with a major in drama. Those who plan to focus on lighting and sound design may take courses in design, electricity, art, history, computers, electronics, mathematics, physics, and sound. Set designers may decide to place their major in architecture. They should take drawing, art and art history, drafting, and sculpture. Makeup artists must know something about anatomy. They also should take sculpture, portrait painting, and other art topics. Most directors, stage managers, and designers earn a Master of Fine Arts degree in drama or another specialty, or a Master of Arts.

On a more personal level, it is important that directors and designers have a strong artistic sense along with the ability to make decisions and instill confidence in others. Managers who are organized, possess strong leadership skills, and can inspire teamwork are bound for success. Stage production workers need to be enthusiastic, energetic, confident, creative, and intelligent. They also need to have a good sense of humor and the ability to handle successes and failures.

## JOB OUTLOOK FOR CAREERS
## BEHIND THE SCENES IN MUSIC

Since the competition for jobs is so fierce for those behind the scenes in music, even seasoned workers have long periods between jobs. Although stage workers do have more steady employment than actors or dancers, many spend weeks and months at other jobs. It is an advantage if you can fill more than one slot, for example, design both sets and props or make and remodel costumes as well as design them. Your chances of getting work will be greater.

## JOB OUTLOOK FOR CAREERS
## BEHIND THE SCENES IN ACTING

Competition is very stiff for behind-the-scenes professionals. Technicians may often be hired as grips (individuals who move equipment such as cameras, etc.) first and work their way up. The emergence of cable television has produced a need for more technicians.

There are possibilities for individuals to become record producers, but only after they have paid their dues and built their knowledge and reputations. Once this happens, producers can go to other labels that are more prestigious and pay higher salaries.

## SALARIES FOR CAREERS BEHIND THE SCENES IN MUSIC

Sound technicians working for a local band that is just getting started may earn only minimum wage or even less. As an average, however, sound technicians earn from about $15,000 to $45,000 or more each year. Higher salaries will go to sound technicians who accompany better-known groups on the road. (It is also important to realize that if the sound technician is a freelancer, he or she may well not work every week.)

Earnings and benefits vary widely depending on the location, medium, and experience of the individual. The following represent typical averages:

broadcast technicians in radio—$440 per week
broadcast technicians in television—$500 per week
sound crew members—$500 to $600 per week for eight performances
  (New York)
beginning sound mixers—$700 to $800 per week
mixers with experience—$1,400 per week
sound recordists—$840 per week
stage manager—$12,000 to $40,000 and up
music video producers, entry-level trainee—$16,000 to $18,000
experienced music video producers—$35,000 to $40,000
producers with own companies—$100,000 to $300,000

Staff record producers may be entitled to a salary plus royalties on the numbers of records produced. This may amount to $18,000 to $45,000 per year and up. Those who freelance will probably be paid a fee by the artist or the record label, again in addition to royalties on works produced. Terms will vary considerably depending on who you are and what your established reputation is. It is possible for a record producer to earn in excess of $250,000 per year.

## SALARIES FOR CAREERS BEHIND THE SCENES IN ACTING

Earnings of stage directors vary greatly. According to the Society of Stage Directors and Choreographers, summer theaters offer compensation including royalties, which are based on the number of performances, usually ranging from $2,000 to $8,000 for a three- to four-week run of a production. Directing a production at a dinner theater will usually pay less than a summer theater, but it has more potential for royalties. Regional theaters may hire directors for longer periods of time, increasing compensation accordingly. The highest paid directors work on Broadway productions, typically earning $80,000 plus royalties.

The following figures represent sample rates for summer theater jobs:

stage directors—$500 to $2,500 a show

stage managers—$150 to $350 per week
costume designers—$500 to $1,500 a show
set designers—$350 to $1,000 or more for each design
lighting and sound designers—$110 to $330 or more per week
property coordinators—$110 to $200 or more per week

technical directors—$110 to $220 or more
painters, carpenters, electricians—$110 to $330 or more
wardrobe workers—$100 to $150 or more

Nearly all stage production workers belong to one or more unions. In New York City, Broadway and off-Broadway workers must belong to a union. In other locations the requirements vary. Actors' Equity Association is a large, strong union to which actors and stage managers belong. Some theaters will only employ Equity actors or Equity stage managers.

Behind-the-scenes workers may be paid by the week, month, or season. Those who are truly skilled at what they do often get much more than a minimum amount. For example, though most riggers earn about $15 per hour, one who is experienced might get $3,000 for a single rock concert.

Sometime summer theaters offer internships with a modest stipend. Some summer programs offer $500 to $900 for the season to assistant designers, stage managers, and technical directors. Technical production interns and shop assistants may be offered $75 per week.

Beginning broadcast technicians in radio and television stations earn from $190 to $330 per week. Experienced technicians earn $330 to $1,000 per week. Union technicians are entitled to union scale.

## PROFILES

### Meet Ross Norton

Ross Norton's educational background includes an associate's degree in instructional technology from the University of Phoenix. Work experience includes positions as production/stage manager, backline/guitar technician, and lighting systems technician in Nashville, Tennessee.

"I always wanted to be close to the music," says Norton. "As a teenager I was a regular concertgoer and found myself always wanting more. I felt that making a living working around something that gave me so much pleasure was the best of both worlds.

"Over the years I have acquired quite a few different job descriptions as the need arose. I originally started out with a lighting company that leased out lights and crews to go with them to different bands touring the circuit of major venues. I now do stage managing and production and was recently the site coordinator for Country Fest '96 in Atlanta.

"Lighting presents a kind of work that is definitely the most brutal. The gear is awkward and heavy. The work hours are long, thankless, and dirty, and the pay for a beginner is next to nothing. Lights are always the first in and the last out, and you will earn every nickel of spare time that you can find. There is no glamour and never has been to this kind of lifestyle. Lighting technicians are definitely the hardest working and most durable of all touring personnel.

"It does, however, provide you with a foot in the door to an otherwise closed room. It will allow you to get a glimpse of how things work at a show to help you decide if you want to work in this industry.

"It won't seem like it at first, but all shows are basically run the same. A typical day starts weeks in advance with calls from the band's production manager to the local promoter who is sponsoring the show. This is called advance work, and how well it's done can definitely affect your day. This is where the number of stage hands (local boys and girls brought in to help the road crew) is decided and all the stage and rigging requirements are hashed out so there will be as few surprises as possible when the trucks arrive. Each lighting and sound configuration is different with each band. Every single cable, chain, and bulb is brought in by the band, unless otherwise ordered. (And when we leave, nothing is left but dust and an empty stage.)

"The trucks usually arrive around eight or nine in the morning, and you are paying for the local crew whether you use them or not, so you had best be quick. The riggers will climb up into the ceiling of the venue and begin hanging points. These are motors that hoist up the lights and sound above the stage. The lighting crew will begin assembling the lighting rig on the stage. A good stage manager will already have checked out the condition of the stage to make sure that it is level, big enough (as per your advance work), and has no weak spots that could cave as gear is added to it. While the lights are being assembled on stage, the sound PA is being unloaded and pushed (as all the gear is) out to the floor in front of the stage. This push could be a matter of feet or, in some cases, a hundred yards through an alley and up to a window on the second floor. It just depends on the building and what it has available.

"There are three distinct and different crews that make up a tour: the lighting crew, sound crew, and the band's personal band crew who set up and take care of their band gear, guitars, etc. These band-aides, as they are sometimes called, also include the production manager, stage manager, and overall tour manager who usually travels with the band and deals with all of their needs.

"The call for band crew is usually around noon or one o'clock. They are the last in and the first out, which can definitely cause tension. After all, the rest of the crew has been hard at work for quite a while. Once the band gear is placed and checked, lights focused, and sound gear tested, we have what is known as a sound check. This usually happens around three in the afternoon and can run anywhere from ten minutes to three hours. Sometimes the band crew, usually musicians themselves, will play the gear for this. If not, this can make for an ugly sound check for those forced to listen. By five in the evening the lights are done, providing they all worked. This is not to be held against the light crew. The gear is delicate and being trucked and handled on a daily basis takes its toll on even the toughest of gear. The PA is up and running now, and if you think you can take a break, you're wrong. The opening act has yet to set up and all of their gear has to be miked, tested, and a sound check conducted. Band gear, stage monitors, and other equipment will all have to be struck from the stage or moved to accommodate the new gear so that there is room for the act. This is usually finished and wrapped up around seven or so in the evening. Doors to the house are now open, and any work you have to do at this point is done with the crowd present. Fun, huh?

"Depending on your job, you may have to work during the show. The band crew will be all over the stage changing guitars as well as at least one senior light technician. Anything that breaks during the show, you have to fix during the show. This is the most stressful on the band crew because though you might be able to do the show with a few less lights, it's pretty hard to pull off the show if the lead guitar rig goes down. A couple of screwups by the band crew during a show usually gets you an early plane ticket home. Any production manager worth his salt has got a long list of band gear technicians who are always ready to replace you for less money than what you are making.

"Once the show is over, you are moving quickly. You could have as much as two to ten tractor trailers full of gear hanging from the roof or on the stage, and it all has to come down and be loaded. This is the hardest part of the day because it is a fast and furious pace and road crews take exceptional pride in their load out times. Usually by two in the morning, the gear is back on the trucks and the crew bus is waiting. Now it is on to the next city because the next show loads in at eight in the morning. Enjoy.

"Throughout the entire day, there is an unseen dance going on between stage hands, lighting and sound crew, as well as the band crew and promoter representatives. Everyone knows the dance and performs it without even thinking, until a new face shows up that hasn't danced before. The truth is that inexperienced people can cause more damage and bodily harm than any other single factor on the road. They trip over cables and even guitars. They put things where they don't belong, don't know who to ask for help, and are usually in the way. If you are new on the road, keep a low profile—that means that you stay low and let us make the profile—and do EXACTLY what you are told. As the years go by, you will learn the dance and hopefully won't have gotten anybody killed in the process. You also will learn who not to talk to during the day. Most road people have been doing this sort of thing for years and know everyone at the halls you will be playing. They have earned a reputation, some good and some bad, but no one wants to hear from the new kid. The day is too short and the hours too long. Ask a million questions to your immediate supervisor, but that is about the length of it in the beginning. Watch and learn. Nothing is done without a reason, no matter how trivial it may seem. There just isn't time for anything else.

"We get an incredible feeling from seeing and hearing a crowd jump on it's feet and scream. It's our job satisfaction to know that without us, none of it would have been possible. The best way to make the impossible happen with us is to tell us that it can't be done. Not only will we show you that it can, but it can be done better than you had hoped. We don't get our names in lights and don't care. There is no limousine waiting for us. We don't want to be stars or hang out with stars. We just do our job and go home to the family. We don't broadcast to people what we do for a living because we don't want to answer the same dumb question every place we go. What's it like? What's it like? What's it like? The answer is, we simply love what we do.

## Meet Randall Presswood

Randall Presswood serves as director of the performing arts facilities for Bloomsburg University in Bloomsburg, Pennsylvania. He earned a Bachelor of Arts in technical theatre from COE College in Cedar Rapids, Iowa, and an M.F.A in theatre design/lighting from Wayne State University. He served his internship as assistant technical director at the Chelsea Theatre Center in New York City.

"My theater 'bug' developed from having performed and worked in the technical aspect of theater at my high school in Wentzville, Missouri," Presswood says. "I enjoyed the challenge of solving technical problems for short-run productions that would enthrall, dazzle, or amaze the audiences. I delighted in seeing the satisfaction and joy on the faces of the audiences as they left the theater. I enjoyed the recognition I received for being part of a successful production and the great comfort and camaraderie I received from my 'extended family.' I knew that what I felt is what I wanted for the audiences that came to my productions. I believe that theater gave me the opportunity to make a small statement to society and perhaps to make a positive impact on the lives of those who witnessed my efforts. It wasn't necessary for them to know that I had a part in this process; it was enough for me to know.

"Choosing theater as a career and lifestyle would allow me to experience this feeling day-in and day-out. For me, there was clearly no other choice.

"Now, as the director of a performing arts facility, I not only have the opportunity to provide this joy for the patrons of my own productions, but I am able to provide a venue for other theater professionals and amateurs alike to present their work to the public. Thus I am able to continue this cycle of escape and entertainment; allowing others to fulfill their dream of providing joy for the theatergoing public.

"I enjoyed the creativity offered me in technical theater—particularly lighting design—more than I did performing. So I decided to study lighting design with the dream of one day accepting the Tony for outstanding lighting design (I still have my acceptance speech ready). I designed for the college and university I attended as much as possible, and I insisted that I be allowed to design a production, for no additional pay, each time I took a summer job as a theater technician/gofer. As I studied the field, I did everything I could—performing, designing, assisting, drafting—to enhance my experiences. My intent was just to be a part of any type of theater that was happening wherever I was. As a result, I received a tremendous amount of education and experience. I learned what was needed as an actor to find the light, what was needed to produce the light as a designer and electrician, and what was needed to make scenery safe, secure, pleasing, and exciting. I also learned what was needed to produce a costume on the stage and what was necessary to manage the stage during a production run. Everything I did added to a total education that has made it possible for me to conduct the business of directing a performing arts facility.

"After receiving my Master of Fine Arts degree in lighting, I accepted a position as a university technical director with lighting design responsibilities. One of my first responsibilities was to refurbish the production shop of this university. I had to research and specify the replacement/purchase of all hand and stationary/portable power tools. Later (for this same university), I was charged to design a student computer laboratory and refurbish the rigging, sound systems, lighting instrumentation, and lighting control, as well as design a production space for a summer dinner theater (complete with preparation kitchen and wet bar). What a wonderful world this opened up for me! I was no longer confined to the benefits of only my designs, but now every designer who ventured after me would benefit from my planning and specifications.

"When I left this university in upstate New York, I sought out an opportunity to continue with facilities refurbishing. What I found instead was a performing arts center just under construction in Northern California. Being hired as the production manager, I was responsible for the production shop from the ground up. (It was literally four walls when I arrived.) Every tool and cabinet was of my specification. The center had hired a theater consultant and sound consultant to assist in the construction of the facility. So although I was not responsible for specifying lighting or sound, my association with these consultants was again a tremendous learning opportunity. My knowledge base was growing by leaps and bounds. I was now familiar and experienced with lighting systems, stage carpentry, electrical needs, safety and fire codes, security needs and applications, budgets, savings methods, personnel and employment procedures, janitorial methods, supplies, and much more. I had developed a large vendor file and was able to make quick and efficient deals; in short, I was building a reputation, not a world-renowned one as I had hoped to forge on Broadway as a lighting designer, but a regional one as a manager who could get the job done. I freelanced as a lighting designer, scenic designer, costumer, and joined Actors' Equity Association as a stage manager.

"As production manager for the center in California, I scheduled the facilities for in-house productions as well as outside rentals. I created the policies and procedures that outside groups would follow and use in their facilities. Eventually I began to field calls from other regional centers in the area wanting to know how I handled this situation or that one, where they should buy this type of hardware, who is the best supplier for lighting equipment, etc. My name continued to grow. I was no longer a lighting designer, but now a theatre designer.

"When I left California, I knew that I would have to continue in my new career—theater design. It's not that my career path had changed (after all, I was still a working theater professional), but it had evolved into what I had actually been trained for. All of my experiences contributed to one another, and my path as a theater designer (in hindsight) only seemed inevitable. It is these experiences, as much as my training, that landed me in my current position in central Pennsylvania as the director of the performing arts facilities for Bloomsburg University.

"I am fortunate that in my present position, my supervisors understand the impact and needs of my position. They assist me in helping them present more opportunities for the users of my facilities. It is not a piece of cake, however.

"I spend a great deal of time scheduling the facilities I direct for the many users wishing access. I am charged by my superiors to provide the most opportunities possible. I run two venues—a 600-seat hall and 2,000-seat hall—and I average four classes and four performances/dress rehearsals per day in my facilities (scheduled a year in advance). I often have to determine the needs of these users, as they may well be novices in the theater and not only unfamiliar with theatrical terminology, but unaware of what can be accomplished in a producing venue. I have to tread the fine line of not offering too much, which in so doing might overwhelm the user, but offering enough so as to provide for the user the best production possible. As the facility director, I am required to review each technical rider for outside presenters/touring groups being produced by the institution. I may choose to contact the proposed group and negotiate the technical needs of the presentation. Although much of this can be accomplished through e-mail and other electronic means, it can, nonetheless, become quite time consuming.

"Depending upon the performance season, I employ twelve to thirty assistants. Each of these employees must be trained in the general theatrical amenities of my facilities, as well as the specific control and operation of facility technology such as lighting and sound and procedures and policies for my department and the institution as a whole. The security of my equipment, the safety of my employees, and the safety of the users and patrons are dependent upon the knowledge I provide these employees.

Because of the time demands on my venues, this training is often done at the performances, which then requires my attendance. It is not unusual to work an eighteen-hour day, or to work four to six weeks straight without a full day off. It would be typical to be called in for an hour or two during a weekend off. The general workday, however, would be about eight to ten hours daily, Monday through Friday. A well-trained staff will determine the availability of my time off.

"As an administrator, I spend between four and eight hours per week in meetings. It is expected that I will likewise spend time contributing to the community.

"Another large portion of my day (and, in fact, that which consumes most of my thoughts while away from the office), is spent planning for improvements, facility rehabilitation, equipment upgrades and replacement, and general maintenance. Since much of this work must be performed by professionals and union tradespeople, a good deal of advance planning and paperwork is required. I must anticipate my needs and my facility/equipment failures in order to schedule these around rentals and productions that are generating income for the institution. To accomplish this, I must spend time researching and keeping abreast of current and proposed technology and theater trends and attend workshops, seminars, and conferences to gain this knowledge. This planning then increases my employee base as I become the site supervisor for the contractors hired to complete the projects placed into the schedule. Gaining the funding for these projects may require grant writing.

"Of course, while all of this work and preparation is going on, the eight events per day are continuing. And everything in my job is deadline based. The stage must be cleared and set by a certain time, the lights must be focused and cued by an exact time, etc. The audience will enter the doors at 6:00 P.M. whether you are prepared for them or not. Consequently, you simply must be prepared, no matter what, no matter when. I have found that a good sense of humor and the ability to let things roll off your back are essential for an arts facilities director.

"What I like most about my job is its constantly changing nature. Although I may do the same or similar work day after day, it is always for a new client with a new set of needs. The challenges are never ending, and the solution to these challenges carry immediate and gratifying rewards. I am in a visible position. My success results in an increased demand on my time and talents. The more I am able to accomplish in my own venue, the more other venues come to me for advice or consultation. I accept this as a compliment and reward for my hard work. I am particularly pleased to be working for an institution that values my efforts, opinions, and proposals and goes the extra step to secure the funding necessary for me to be successful. This is not always the case, so I feel rewarded to have that support and encouragement.

"Of course, the sometimes relentless hours and the need to occasionally function under crises management are among the dislikes of my job. As an administrator I am sometimes viewed as the obstacle or enemy to those presenting in my venue. It is my job to provide a total experience for many users and patrons. However, each user is convinced that their four hours in my space is the most important thing I will do all year long. When I thoroughly research and propose a project and become convinced that it is an important step for the institution, it is indeed frustrating when I am unable to convince my superiors to accept that belief. Whereas the art of theater is a collaborative one, the business of theater is often tooth and nail.

"If you want to make a living in theater, be prepared to go where the path leads you. Don't force yourself down the straight path when the winding one is tugging at your boot straps. If it is important to you to be a theater professional, then just be in the theater. Don't insist that you become an actor or designer. Be willing and prepared to become a box office manager, stage carpenter, or a director of performing arts facilities."

## Meet Dennis Parichy

Dennis Parichy earned a Bachelor of Science degree in theater from the School of Speech at Northwestern University in Evanston, Illinois. In addition, he completed course work in lighting design, drafting, drawing, and painting for the theater designer at Lester Polakov Studio and Forum of Stage Design. He serves as a professional lighting designer.

"My first designs were for Eagles Mere Playhouse in Eagles Mere, Pennsylvania, a non-Equity summer theater operated by Alvina Krause, Professor of Acting, Northwestern University," says Parichy. "I discovered lighting design in a class in stage lighting during my junior year at Northwestern University and was so fascinated that I asked Miss Krause to take me to Eagles Mere (she took people she judged to be talented and trainable) so that I could try this new field. Previously I had flirted with writing plays, acting (too self-conscious), and technical theater, about which I knew very little. So since lighting seemed an important and fascinating area of theater, I wanted to try my hand at it. Working at Eagles Mere— nine shows in ten weeks—I was electrician as well as designer, without any supervision or help from the directors. Consequently, I had to take the ideas lighting class had given me about technique and craft, with the injunction to support and illuminate the play, and try to work out how to light each show effectively and artistically. This included a substantial amount of trial and error in addition to putting Professor Theodore Fuch's teachings into practice. The only experience I had had before this was working on the lighting crew of a couple of university productions.

"In the course of three summers, I learned an enormous amount about turning lighting ideas into effective designs. I had to test each idea I had acquired, figure out how to make it work with very limited resources, find out what worked and what did not, and discover my own lighting preferences. It was, of course, a high-pressure situation guided only by my own insights and the needs of the moment. Compared to formal training, it was chaotic, but it gave me invaluable experience about the realities of achieving a lighting design. I was able to learn firsthand how you must light the actors and the space effectively in order to achieve the basic goal of making the theatrical performance visible to the audience in a way that helps them understand and relate to the onstage events.

"For several years I had an interest in astronomy, physics, and engineering as possible careers. All of these areas fascinated me, though I never felt I had the necessary drive and kind of mind that could carry me very far in those professions. But looking back, I would say that those interests predisposed me to find lighting design, with its apparent technical aspects—control, instrumentation, optics, color, etc.—all concrete and gadgetlike things—a familiar and exciting field. The other influence was totally nontechnical: a great fascination with books—primarily stories, novels, adventures, etc.—that briefly led me into playwriting. I had an interest in stories and the telling of stories, which is what theater does. So theater design, and specifically lighting, combined an interest in technical and scientific things with the opportunity to help tell fascinating stories about people's experiences—to put those technical things in the service of creating art.

"Once the rudiments of technique are acquired, lighting design involves the ability to delve into the nature of a script, libretto, score, or choreography; open your mind to what it is, what it means, and what emotions, images, and ideas it evokes in you; and translate those things into ideas about color, direction, and intensity of light. The job has four major components:

1. Experiencing the work. This includes reading a script, listening to a score, and/or watching a rehearsal in order to experience the work for yourself in some vivid and immediate way. It means exploring the ideas, images, and emotions this experience arouses for you and developing your own point of view about the piece at hand. The process may require a single reading/listening or a dozen or more, depending on the particular show, its complexity and demands, and your own interests and needs.

2. Discussing the work. The next stage focuses on discussions with the show's director and/or producer, the other designers, and anyone else involved in creating the overall production. This usually requires several meetings or phone conversations with one or more of your fellow collaborators, all in pursuit of defining the needs of this particular production regarding lighting, scenic, costume, and directorial elements. The goal is to produce a unified approach to the play in which the lighting design will blend with and support the work of everyone else. This process takes place over the course of several weeks.

3. Arranging the lighting instruments. Once the first two steps are well underway (they may continue and overlap with later stages of your work), you take the ideas and needs and points of view about the show and sit down at the drafting table, desk, and computer and figure out (in very specific terms) how to arrange lighting instruments in the theater space to create the kind of look that you and the director have decided the show needs. This means analyzing the scenic elements; the physical reality of the theater; the money, time, and resources available to you; and determining and solving the inherent problems in this particular situation. During this part of the process, you have to decide what kind of lights you need (or how to use those that are available), where to put them, where they will be focused, how to control them, and what color and intensity they must have in order to achieve your goals. The designer then has to produce a light plot, hookup, shop order, and other lists and specifications that will communicate to the crew what is needed, where it should be located in the theater, and how it will be wired and equipped. This part of the job may be done by the designer in the studio (or with assistants), can last anywhere from a day or two to three weeks (for a large and complex show), and may require constant consultation with the

producers, managers, and the shops that supply the equipment and the workers who do the installation.

4. Creating the lighting. The last phase of lighting design is the actual week to several weeks you spend in the theater creating the specific lighting and executing the design in order to make the show have the look all have decided upon. This begins when the lights are hung and includes focusing the lights, creating the looks of the show (the cues), rehearsing the show, and modifying and refining the looks so that they all help the audience experience the show. Usually this period lasts from two to three days for summer stock to about ten days for most regional theater shows and plays. However, in the case of new and complex musicals, the time required may be several weeks (putting in twelve-hour days, six-day weeks).

"A typical day is difficult to spell out since every show has its own schedule, needs, and special circumstances. In the professional theater, most designers are in the process of designing several shows at once, each at a different stage of the process. So a typical day might easily involve working in the studio in the morning on the light plot or hookup of a show you are going to do in two or three weeks. Then in the afternoon you might go to a run-through of the show that you will light next week. During the rehearsal, you note important things about cuing and staging that must be taken into account. You may discuss specific cues, problems, or needs with the stage manager and director. At the end of rehearsal, you might be required to attend a production meeting about a show that you will do two months from now and discuss with the director and perhaps other designers various ideas about that show, what its story is, and what it should look like. And then in the evening—if you're very busy—and the schedule is tight—as it often is—you go home and read the script for another show, think about the show just discussed, or go to the theater and begin focusing next week's show (till midnight typically).

"There are, of course, an infinite number of variations on this schedule. The designer is required to take control of his or her work and be self-motivated, independent, dedicated, and ambitious. You have to get the job done, and no one is supervising you.

"The work, while you're working, is intense, often tense, and driven by deadlines. The plot has to be delivered on time, the lights have to go in the theater on a specific day, and there can be no postponements. You have to be ready and you have to be willing and able to work under pressure and to take charge. Once in a while it is relaxed and easygoing, but that is the exception. Most lighting designers, in order to make a good living, take on as many shows as they can possibly work into their schedules, so high-pressure, anxiety, and stress are an inevitable part of the experience.

"I have often had the privilege and opportunity to work with playwrights, directors, designers, and actors who welcome my contribution and with whom I have forged lasting personal and artistic relationships. But sometimes shows are fraught with disagreement, demands, and unhappiness, and these situations can be stressful and exhausting. Each show is a new challenge and adventure.

"What I like most about my work is the chance to help create an effective theatrical event in collaboration with other eager, exciting, and stimulating theater artists. The process of creating the design—especially the days in the theater—is almost always an exciting and satisfying time, because it gives me a chance to exercise my skills and visual talents, which is immensely satisfying. The process—from show to show—may be bumpy or difficult or fraught with occasional conflict, but it is almost always in the end such a source of fulfillment, that this makes the difficulties acceptable.

"The downside of lighting design (applicable I believe to almost all theatrical careers) is that there is often a lack of continuity, security, and stability in theatrical work. No matter how advanced your career, there is always the possibility that you may have to struggle for sufficient work to support yourself and a family; as associates and colleagues move on in their careers, you may have to unexpectedly develop new relationships and find new sources of work. Since the network of friends and professional colleagues—especially directors—is extremely important to one's success, you are often vulnerable to significant changes in your relationships with theaters and other theater artists. At some point, finding work that will stimulate and stretch your artistic muscles may be difficult, and you have to be continually aware of the need to escape from the typecasting that inevitably happens.

"I think the most important advice I could give someone interested in lighting design as a career is to be realistic about the likely monetary and artistic rewards of lighting design in the theater. If you have the dedication, drive, and ambition to tackle the professional world; to put in the inevitable apprenticeship of learning the ropes and living hand-to-mouth for a while, you have a chance. If you are determined to do it and are willing to brave the rigors of finding your niche, you have a good chance of succeeding. Training is important, but dedication and enthusiasm; a willingness to learn and expand; a genuine enjoyment of and eagerness to work with and for others, and an effort to submit your artistic impulses to the needs and demands of the production are what will make you a success.

### Meet Joseph Hayes

Joseph Hayes has worked as a sound technician for theater, television, and radio for the past twenty years. He earned his Bachelor of Arts degree from Lehman College in New York.

"I started my career as a working musician, both as a solo and with bands. Immediately I found that the best way to protect the quality of my sound was to learn how to do it myself.

"I like the feeling of immediate accomplishment, when a show goes well, or an audience is shocked, pleased, roused, or lulled immediately by the sound of the performance.

"In television, jobs are usually boring, with long hours of waiting to shoot. However, in theater, there is always something to do. There are enormously long days of pre-show set up. Sometimes this means twelve- or fourteen-hour days of cabling, testing, and fine-tuning. In a complicated performance—for example, this year's Orlando Shakespeare Festival, which involved twenty-four speaking parts, all with microphones and countless prerecorded sound cues—the sound operator is constantly busy, and one miscue or late microphone is noticed immediately. Unlike lighting people, who wait for cues from the stage manager, the soundperson has to always be conscious of the show.

"I love the feeling of a job well done, and I do my job well. It is very satisfying to hear an audience gasp when a sudden drum rings out. Like writing, theater tech work depends entirely on one's own abilities. There is no faking it on this job.

"The least satisfying aspects of the job are the hours, the gaps between work, having to deal with those actors who don't understand the complexities of what I do (and tell you how easy you have it), and having to listen to those who refer to me as 'only a tech' (who are fortunately in the minority). Most actors appreciate tremendously the fact that you are making them look (and sound) good.

"My advice to anyone considering this field is to work—work hard. See as many professional performances as you can. Ask questions. Volunteer at a local community theater. Talk to the old-timers. Organized education is wonderful, but a degree in sound only gets you so far. It's the doing that counts."

## FOR MORE INFORMATION

The following companies and associations can provide additional information and possibilities for career advancement.

Acoustical Society of America (ASA)
500 Sunnyside Boulevard
Woodbury, NY 11797

American Theater Works, Inc.
Theater Directories
P.O. Box 519
Dorset, VT 05251

Arista Records
6 West Fifty-Seventh Street
New York, NY 10019
Contact: Human Resources

Association for Communication
Administration
ACA National Office
311 Wilson Hall
Murray State University
Murray, KY 42071

Broadcast Education Association
National Association of
Broadcasters
1771 N Street, NW
Washington, DC 20006

Cleopatra Records
P.O. Box 1394
Hollywood, CA 90078

(The) Commercial Theatre Institute
250 West Fifty-Seventh Street,
Suite 1818
New York, NY 10107

International Alliance of Theatrical
Stage Employees (IATSE)
Local 33 IATSE
1720 West Magnolia Boulevard
Burbank, CA 91506

International Association of
Auditorium Managers (IAAM)
4425 West Airport Freeway
Irving, TX 75062

International Brotherhood of
Electrical Workers (IBEW)
1125 Fifteenth Street, NW
Washington, DC 20005

League of American Theaters
and Producers
226 West Forty-Seventh Street
New York, NY 10036

League of Professional Theater
Women/New York
c/o Shari Upbin Productions
300 East Fifty-Sixth Street
New York, NY 10022

National Association of Broadcasters
   Employment Clearinghouse
   1771 N Street, NW
   Washington, DC 20036

National Association of Schools
   of Theater
   11250 Roger Bacon Drive, Suite 21
   Reston, VA 22090

SONY Music and Entertainment, Inc.
   550 Madison Avenue, 2nd Floor
   New York, NY 10022-3211
   Contact: Recruitment Department

## CHAPTER 5

# THE BUSINESS OF ENTERTAINMENT

If you want a place in the sun, you have to expect a few blisters.
—Loretta Young, quoted in John Robert Colombo's
*Popcorn in Paradise*

In the world at large, the art of negotiation by a third party has been in existence ever since individuals began communicating with one another. This job of facilitator was historically given to the individual who, for a fee, would arrange an audience with important officials (or royalty) or set up a meeting for those seeking a face-to-face encounter. Today, in the world of entertainment, that job is often handled by individuals called personal managers, business managers, booking agents, or artists' agents who act as representatives and negotiators for their clients.

Are you knowledgeable about the world of music but not comfortable actually performing? Do you have a desire to handle the business end of things? Can you speak persuasively? Are you good with figures? Perhaps you might be interested in becoming an artist's representative, personal manager, or booking agent.

### ARTISTS' REPRESENTATIVES OR
### PERSONAL/BUSINESS MANAGERS

Personal managers, also called artists' representatives or agents, are responsible for representing artists. Their specific responsibilities may vary but, in many cases, they are in charge of all aspects of a performer's career, promoting their client's interests whenever and wherever possible. This includes business decisions and also may include all or some creative decisions.

Agents may represent many artists at one time. Sometimes agents specialize and represent only one type of performer or even one type of music, such as rock music. They may work for a large or small agency or be self-employed.

Much of an agent's time is spent on the phone, FAX, or e-mail discussing prospects, arranging meetings, making networking connections, and keeping in touch with what is going on in the industry.

One of the most important jobs for agents is to negotiate contracts. Other duties include seeing to and improving costuming, choreography, backup musicians and tunes, as well as arranging publicity and providing guidance for their clients. If the entertainer is well established, the manager may be in charge of support personnel including publicists or public relations firms, road personnel, security people, accountants, producers, musicians, and merchandisers. Successful managers are always in constant communication with the act's booking agent or agency.

Booking agents are also called theatrical agents, booking managers, booking representatives, agents, or bookers. These professionals are in charge of arranging engagements for both solo musical artists and/or groups for movies, television programming, concerts, and live performances. They usually represent a number of clients at a time. Sometimes they are chosen to act as talent buyers for concert halls or clubs or may open their own talent agency.

Business managers concentrate on the financial affairs of the singers, musicians, and other entertainers whom they represent. They are often the ones who negotiate with agents or representatives for contracts and appearances. They may also negotiate with television producers, record companies, and motion picture studios and sometimes seek large endorsements of concert tours. They are in charge of all fiscal disbursements, making sure the bills are in order and that the payroll for all employees in the act (including road personnel, musicians, vocalists, publicists, public relations firms, lawyers, etc.) is dispensed properly. Business managers may even be in charge of the artist's personal bills.

## PRODUCERS

Producers are entrepreneurs who have financial and administrative control over the making of movies, plays, and television shows. It is their responsibility to raise enough money, oversee all finances, and make sure that all dollars are wisely spent. They must find investors (called *angels*) who are willing to put up money to finance the project. They are the ones who are ultimately responsible for turning a profit for the investors. The producer is also responsible for selecting the plays or scripts, deciding on the size and content of the production, and its budget.

Scripts may be located in a number of ways: playwrights may send them to producers, sometimes producers might also do new versions of previous productions, and often the producer may commission a playwright to write a script. Once a script is located or written, the producer will pay the playwright for an option to use the script for a specified time period.

Producers hire directors who make the artistic and day-to-day decisions on the production. They also choose the principal members of the cast and key production staff members. They may negotiate contracts with artistic personnel (often in accordance with collective bargaining agreements) and coordinate the activities of writers, directors, managers, and other personnel. Producers have many responsibilities; ultimately they are the ones who make the decisions that determine the success of the project.

Television producers are employed by television stations or networks. Network television series usually have an executive producer who does the long-term planning for the show. Movie producers are employed by a film studio or may work independently. Theatrical producers work independently.

## CASTING DIRECTORS

Casting directors are influential theater professionals who audition and interview performers for specific parts in a play or movie. In order to correctly match people with parts, casting directors read scripts and then work with others in the production staff to determine their thoughts, ideas, and desires regarding the character's personality, voice quality, and physical appearance.

Casting directors may find the right performer in a number of ways. They develop advertisements and place them in the trades, newspapers, or other publications. These ads announce casting requirements of the production. They may also hold open auditions, where hundreds or even thousands of hopeful actors and actresses come to audition for parts. Most casting directors also have a file of information on all the performers who ever auditioned for them, as well as a file on those who have sent resumes and photos but never formally auditioned.

In some cases, established actors or actresses hear about a production, are interested in a specific role, and instruct their agents to call the casting director. If these well-known actors and actresses are very successful in the industry and are right for the part, they will often get a role without auditioning. Similarly, casting directors might have a specific actor or actress in mind for a part. In these instances, they contact the performer's agent to check out the interest and availability.

Often casting directors and actors meet in a *pre-read session.* Usually this includes about twenty people who are in contention for the part. The purpose of the meeting is to screen out people so that the producer's time is not wasted unnecessarily. From the twenty, usually, five or six candidates are chosen to bring to a *producer's session,* which also includes the casting director.

Internships always provide invaluable education and experience. As a casting director's intern, one of your important responsibilities might be to take care of calls from producers and directors. You also might be involved in casting a TV show, which would require that you spend your days reading a script in order to determine the list of characters needed to fill these parts. Then you might send the list to agents (possibly also to a service that forwards them to agents and managers) who will subsequently send you submissions (envelopes with pictures and resumes of candidates) to fill these roles. Then you'd pick out the people to audition.

## GENERAL MANAGERS

General managers are the individuals in charge of legal details. They may set up the play company as a corporation and also negotiate contracts with those who have been hired to be part of the production. They may aid in preparing budgets and make sure that costs stay within them. It is their job to set ticket prices, hire a company manager, and order the printed tickets.

## COMPANY MANAGERS

Company managers are in charge of making out the payroll and seeing to it that appropriate taxes are paid. They also work with box office managers on receipts and ticket sales. Once the show is closed, they make sure that nothing remains in the theater.

## BOX OFFICE MANAGERS

Box office managers are strictly in charge of tickets. It is their job to arrange the sales of tickets through mail order, advance ticket sales at the theater, and any other outlets they have in mind. They are held accountable for all ticket sales and money derived from them.

## HOUSE MANAGERS

House managers are responsible for the upkeep of the theater. As a result, they must be present whenever anyone else is there. They are also in charge of ushers, fire and safety laws, and extra stagehands who are hired to move the sets into and out of the theater.

## TOURING PRODUCTION MANAGERS

When the show is on the road, touring production managers are in charge of all business affairs of the company. Their duties usually include obtaining local permits, hiring local stagehands, arranging for housing for the cast and other members of the staff, and working with local unions. They also audit box office accounts and write out and disburse paychecks.

## THEATRICAL PRESS AGENTS

Theatrical press agents are the professionals in charge of handling all of the publicity for regional theater group productions, off-Broadway shows, and Broadway shows. If a show is going to be successful, it is imperative that enough publicity is given so that sufficient ticket sales will be generated. In order to accomplish this, theatrical press agents must create press kits, prepare biographies, write press releases, arrange interviews, and deal with all media sources.

For this job it is critical to make the right media contacts. This entails compiling lists that will be used to send press releases, press passes, and perhaps invitations for opening night. Along with this, the theatrical press agent must plan as many events and press conferences as possible to generate as much publicity as possible. It is important that these professionals are creative about developing new ideas and new angles for exposure through reporters, entertainment and feature writers, and other newspaper and magazine writers.

Opening night is a gala event that theatrical press agents are in charge of. It is their responsibility to call all reviewers and critics on the day of the show to make sure they will be present in the audience. The agents will be on hand on the day of the opening to be the liaison to the media, pass out press kits, or provide any information that is required.

## TRAINING FOR THE BUSINESS OF ENTERTAINMENT IN MUSIC

Though there are no specific educational requirements for many of these careers in the music business, a college degree with a broad arts and sciences background and a focus on music or at least course work including management, communications, contracts and contract law, journalism, law, business, and music is definitely helpful for success. Possessing a broad range of knowledge about music and the music industry is very important.

On-the-job training will bring the experience needed to promote you in the field. Agents who make arrangements to represent musicians or singers will get a substantial knowledge of the industry through performing in a musical group or working in a recording studio themselves. This also helps to build another important asset—contacts in the music industry—the more, the better.

Desirable personal qualities include salesmanship, good public relations skills; assertiveness (aggressiveness), strong communications skills, excellent phone presence, patience, and perseverance. In addition the ability to evaluate and recognize exceptional talent, provide constructive advice, work well with people, gain clients and find appropriate work for them, negotiate successfully, and work at a fast pace and under great pressure are invaluable.

For record producers, the most important ability is skill in choosing records that will appeal to many people. A number-one hit song is the greatest goal, of course. Thus, successful record producers must be so familiar and comfortable with sound and songs that they are able to pick songs that will do well on the charts. It is important that they can recognize raw talent that can be cultivated when combined with excellent arranging and high-quality recording devices.

Business managers need to be cognizant of investments and money strategies.

## TRAINING FOR THE BUSINESS OF ENTERTAINMENT IN ACTING

No standard educational or training requirements exist for producers and other business theater professionals. However, a thorough knowledge and understanding of theater is absolutely necessary, and a college degree gives individuals a certain measure of credibility and increased opportunities for hands-on training. Course work should focus on theater, film, business, English, fine arts, law, fiscal management, and personnel management. Advanced degrees are generally not necessary and, as a rule, do not affect earnings. Seminars and workshops in theater and producing are important.

Professionals in this area of theater need good business sense, financial management skills, organizational skills, effective communication skills, strong interpersonal skills, and negotiation skills. They also must have the ability to listen, match people with roles, work under pressure, relate to clients, handle stress, and attend to details.

A three-year apprenticeship with a member of the Association of Theatrical Press Agents and Managers (ATPAM) is required for theatrical press agents. While a college degree is not a requirement, many in the business believe that it is the best approach. Good course choices include public relations, communications, writing, advertising, marketing, business, English, and theater arts. Theatrical press agents must be creative, detail oriented, and aggressive and must have excellent verbal and written communication skills. They need experience in publicity, public relations, or promotion.

## JOB OUTLOOK FOR THE BUSINESS OF
## ENTERTAINMENT IN MUSIC

The outlook for personal managers and booking agents is cautious. In most cases, individuals begin by representing local talent and work their way up to representing more well-known performers. Since one agent can handle many clients, this is a competitive profession that cannot accommodate large numbers of new people. The best opportunities exist in New York City, Los Angeles, or Nashville.

## JOB OUTLOOK FOR THE BUSINESS OF
## ENTERTAINMENT IN ACTING

The number of producers is small and few new ones are hired each year. Theatrical producers work from show to show. For agents, success lies in finding new talent and promoting it in order to earn a reputation and a bigger salary. Competition is fierce among all of these occupations.

Prospective casting directors should be advised that it's almost impossible to get a job in casting without interning first. There are so many people who are willing to work for free as a way to break into Hollywood. Find out about internships by looking in *The Casting Director's Directory,* which is sold at Samuel French bookstore in Los Angeles. It lists the names, addresses, and phone numbers of all the casting directors and what shows they cast. Then send your resume to those of your choice.

Potential theatrical press agents should know that you can acquire much needed experience by handling the publicity and promotion for a school, college, or community theater production. Look for seminars, workshops, and classes in publicity, writing, promotion, and theater. These experiences will improve your skills in addition to providing opportunities to make important contacts.

## SALARIES FOR THE BUSINESS OF
## ENTERTAINMENT IN MUSIC

Personal managers usually receive 10 to 15 percent of an artist's earnings. Often they also receive percentages of merchandise that is sold. They may earn from about $18,000 to $60,000 per year. Naturally, agents wish their clients to be successful because they usually work on a commission basis, and if the clients are popular they will make more money.

Agents for classical musicians usually receive 20 percent for their work in all fields but opera, which receives only a 10 percent commission. In many states talent agents are licensed.

Booking agents usually take anywhere from 10 to 20 percent of the amount the act is being paid for that performance. In some cases, they are paid a salary plus a percentage of the figures they add to the agency. Amounts vary considerably, but at the top they may earn anywhere from $200,000 to $750,000.

Business managers may make $20,000 to $750,000 per year or more. Earnings may be based upon a percentage of the act's total gross income. The percentage varies from 3 to 10 percent.

## SALARIES FOR THE BUSINESS OF ENTERTAINMENT IN ACTING

In general the pay for producers is good but varies due to experience, company, and production budget. Though producers on staff usually receive a specific salary, others do not. Instead, they might receive a finder's fee for putting together a group of investors. Others are compensated with a percentage of the profits earned from the show. Figures for producers can vary from a few thousand to hundreds of thousands of dollars. However, entry-level producers in television usually earn around $20,000 per year. Unionized producers generally receive paid vacation and health insurance.

Because of the nature of the job, it is difficult to determine annual earnings of casting directors. A lot depends on whether professionals are consultants or on staff, the nature of the production, and how many productions they cast each year. For individuals who are on staff, salaries may range from $10,000 to $75,000 or more; consultants may charge $2,000 to $40,000 or more per production.

Agents usually make a standard 10 or 15 percent commission of all of the client's earnings, but actual salaries vary greatly depending on the experience and talent of the individual. Agents working on a part-time basis can earn anywhere from $15,000 to $50,000 a year. Benefits vary.

Agents working for large agencies generally are offered health insurance and paid vacations.

Since individuals are usually hired for specific productions, it's difficult to determine annual earnings for theatrical press agents. Factors affecting this include the number of projects that year, how long the production lasts, and the size and type of theater. Minimum earnings are negotiated by the Association of Theatrical Press Agents and Managers (ATPAM), an AFL-CIO union. Earnings include a minimum weekly salary plus a percentage for pensions, vacation pay, and a set figure for a welfare fund. Theatrical press agents usually earn about $600 to $1,600 per week and up.

## PROFILES

### Meet Bill Hibbler

Bill Hibbler is owner of Texas Funk Syndicate, an artist management company in Houston, Texas. He attended Houston Community College in Houston, Texas.

"I've spent twenty-two years in the trenches," Hibbler says. "I've dealt with vintage guitars, run sound, and handled security, and I've been a backline technician, road manager, stage manager, tour coordinator, disc jockey, program director, and album project coordinator. I have also published music industry directories and conducted seminars and managed artists.

"I was always a big fan of music. As a child, I was always the one who brought the music along. A good friend of mine kept dragging me into music stores to show me the guitar he dreamed of buying. I ended up buying a bass myself, but I was never very good at it and gave up after a while. One night after attending a concert, I spotted the salesman who sold me my bass trying to haul about half a dozen guitar cases into the arena for the headliner's guitar player to check out. My friend and I quickly volunteered to help him carry the guitars in, and he got us each a stage pass. Once backstage I was totally fascinated with the whole scene, meeting the bands and watching this small army of technicians and local stage hands break down the gear.

"After that I was hooked. I spent my afternoons at the venues in the hope that I could help with the instruments or anything else. I freely offered to deliver whatever supplies the crew might need from the music store. Though I didn't make much money, I did get a couple of backstage passes to the show and would get to meet some of my favorite bands. It wasn't easy at first. I'd have a hard time getting past security and into the arenas, but eventually I developed relationships with the local concert promoters who realized that I was providing a service that was useful to everyone involved. Also, by this time, most of the guitar technicians who were on the road had either met me when they'd been to Houston or had heard of me through the grapevine. I used to make sure to bring a few T-shirts and stickers (advertising my company) along, and the stickers would usually find their way onto the bands' flight cases. Word started to get around.

"From the beginning, I knew I wanted to be a road manager. After graduating from high school, I went to college, but I decided to leave to enter the music business. During the next few years, I ran sound for local bands, booked for a small club, managed a stereo store, and worked at Houston's Agora Ballroom doing security and stage work. In 1982 I got my first break and was hired to be a backline technician for Humble Pie. After a few months, there was a change in management and I became the road manager.

"It was an unusual position to be in at the time. In those days there were no schools that offered courses in artist or tour management careers, and it was difficult to access working tour managers. I'd been in contact with these professionals for years at shows, but only briefly, as they were usually very busy. I think the best way to learn this career is to find a mentor and learn what the job is really all about. However, I found myself in the job before finding that mentor. Luckily, I had pretty good instincts, which is important for anyone working on a road crew.

"I spent three great years with Humble Pie before the band broke up. A big mistake I'd made during those years was not developing a better network so that I could find more work. Usually someone in my position would be working for a band with a big management company, booking agent, or record label that would send them out with their other bands or refer them. With Humble Pie, we didn't have that type of management, and the band wasn't signed. Our booking agent specialized in southern rock bands like the Allman Brothers, Charlie Daniels Band, and ARS, and they kept the same individuals, usually relatives or friends from the early years, without hiring a new crew every time they went out (like a large number of European bands did). I couldn't find a tour manager position, so, for several years, I worked as a club disc jockey in Atlanta and later in Houston.

"During that time, I met Glenn Hughes when he was about to go out on tour with Black Sabbath. We became friends and he offered me a job as his assistant on the tour. However, Sabbath's management wanted to use someone else at that time. I finally went to work for Glenn in January of 1995 as the project coordinator for his album, *Feel.* About six months later, Glenn and his Japanese record label asked me to take over as his manager.

"I now manage Glenn along with two local bands and am in discussions right now with another established artist.

"My job can be like a roller coaster ride at times. I have to wear a lot of different hats as a manager, and some days things are a lot more hectic than others. The time leading up to and during a tour is probably the busiest.

"My work schedule varies tremendously but is always centered around the telephone, fax machine, and e-mail. Glenn's primary markets right now are Europe and Japan, so, due to the time difference, I often find myself on the phone as early as 5:00 or 6:00 A.M. During a tour, I might finish up at 9:00 or 10:00 P.M. by dealing with our tour manager after the show. But there are often gaps in the day where I can get away for a couple of hours if there are no emergencies to deal with.

"Things are a lot more laid-back when I direct my attention to studio recording. My initial job is to put a budget together for the album. I'll cut deals with the producer, engineer, and studios for recording, mixing, and mastering; purchase or hire any tape and equipment we'll need; and arrange scheduling, etc. In addition to making arrangements for any supplemental musicians or special guests, I'll take care of arranging photo sessions and meetings with the graphic designer to plan the artwork for both the CD and the marketing materials. (Our label lets us handle a lot of this. Other labels play a much larger role in selecting marketing materials.) During the sessions, I'll be in charge of paying all the bills and tracking expenses. As we get closer to completion, I'll be working with the label to determine promotional plans, schedules, and everything else.

"As to the downsides, I usually enjoy the challenges that arise in the United States, but I find dealing with a European tour to be pretty stressful. It's a lot easier to solve a problem like finding a piece of equipment or a replacement vehicle if the band is here in America where you have easy access to directory assistance and everyone speaks the same language.

Even something as simple as finding super glue late at night in Europe is nearly impossible, (unlike America where there's a twenty-four-hour convenience store on every corner). In addition to all the usual circumstances, you've got to deal with multiple currencies, which makes for budgeting challenges and bookkeeping problems. There are increased costs of doing business in Europe, obviously phone calls are more expensive, and an overnight envelope costs four times as much to ship. Generally everything from hotels to equipment is costlier, and you have to pay value added taxes as high as 25 percent.

On the local scene, I've seen so many musicians who will sit and complain about the city they live in, or cut down a rival band that got signed, but never take the necessary steps to make it happen for themselves. At a higher level, there are the people who can't be bothered to show up on time, do interviews, etc., and they step on a lot of people's toes. They forget about the old adage about being decent to people on your way up because those same people are going to be there on your way back down. Musicians like that can really be a drain on a manager.

"As far as the upsides/downsides from a more business standpoint, it's not that hard to become a manager. These days, for a few thousand dollars, you can put together an office that rivals a big corporation—a computer, modem, printer, telephone, and a couple of phone lines and you're in business. Computers really level the playing field because you can handle your bookkeeping, graphic design, faxing, voice mail, trip planning, and mailing lists, and contact management and do marketing with one machine. With the Internet and on-line services, you can develop a great network, do research, and market your music without ever leaving your apartment.

"One of the big downsides is that being a manager can become a full-time job long before it pays full-time money. Assuming a typical management commission is 15 percent, your artist has to be grossing $80,000 a year before you can earn $1,000 a month. So, at the beginning, it helps to have a day job where you have the ability to make and receive phone calls at work that are band related.

"For those who might be interested in pursuing this type of work, I would first of all suggest that you read as much as you can about the business. You must acquire a feel for how recording, publishing, and merchandising deals are put together; how record companies and publishing companies are organized; and how things fit into place. You don't have to know how to operate recording and stage gear, but it helps to have a good overview of what does what and how the recording process works. And, perhaps most important, you need to learn how to understand all the various contracts you'll encounter.

"There are some excellent schools with music business programs, but many of them do nothing more than give you a bit of a foundation to build on, rather than enabling you to go right to work. The real education comes from the internship that you should serve while attending school. (If you decide to pursue the school route, I'd recommend doing so in Los Angeles or New York. In those cities you'll have a lot more access to the people who make things happen in the music business than if you choose to take a class back home.) Your school can help you with this, and/or you can check on-line services, music industry forums, and magazines like *LA Music Connection,* which has an intern classified section. Many of these internships require you to be in a school program as you'll probably be working for free and the school internship is the only way a company can get around not paying you minimum wage. That's OK at this point because you'll be gaining valuable experience. I like the idea of interning in a smaller company because in a major record label office, you may be stuck doing phone surveys or in the mail room and never get to really see how things are done.

"Whatever way you choose to get a start on your education, you should treat the music business as a science. Forget about the fantasy of having your band getting discovered by some A & R guy who fishes your tape out of a pile of demos or who accidentally stumbles into your show. Set goals, develop a plan for yourself and for your artist, and then take action.

"Besides getting an education, you want to begin developing contacts. It's never too early to start. Keep them in a software program like ACT or Lotus Organizer or in a day planner book. Organize your list of contacts into A, B, and C contacts and prioritize them according to their power and position. Make A the highest level. Call your A-level contacts once every two to three weeks, your B contacts every four to six weeks, and your C contacts once every two to three months, and try to find ways to help them while you're trying to help yourself. Learn to be persistent and don't let the word "no" affect you personally. "No" today could mean "Yes" tomorrow. Keep working on and following your game plan, making adjustments as needed. If you make a mistake, try to learn from it and then move on.

"These days, once you're learned the business, it is entirely possible to find success no matter where you live. Get the right band with the right songs and do what's necessary to release your own CD. Before you release it, follow a preplanned promotional plan and stick to it until you've made a strong impact at your hometown. Once your act has reached that level, choose nearby cities or college towns and apply the same plan of action until you accomplish similar results, and then continue to expand city by city. Before long you'll have a nice little region where you're getting air play at some levels, selling copies of your CD in every city, and are drawing nice crowds to all your shows. Continue to expand in this fashion and the major labels will find you.

"I love to travel, and this business gives me the opportunity to do lots of that, although you often don't get a lot of free time to explore the cities you visit. Still, it's a great adventure. Working in the music business allows me to work at home without facing the boredom of a nine-to-five type job. As a manager, I get to be a part of the big picture and work in a variety of roles. I have friends in the corporate world who are tied to a small section of a huge company. Their role doesn't allow them to see what their contribution is, and their work is often duplicated by three or four other people. The trade-off for this used to be job security, but since this is certainly no longer the case, why not take a risk and do something you love? That's what I did!"

### Meet Gary Murphy

Gary Murphy is an independent publicist specializing in national public relations campaigns for the performing arts. He serves as the national press representative for The Geffen Playhouse in Los Angeles, the Alley Theater in Houston, and Santa Fe Stages in Santa Fe, New Mexico. He earned his Bachelor of Science degree in English education from SUNY at Cortland. Gary did not enter his profession overtly, it just sort of happened.

"In 1977, while recovering from an illness, a friend suggested I tend the intermission bar at Manhattan Theatre Club in New York City as a recuperative activity," says Murphy. "I had recently graduated from college with a teaching degree but found the idea of actually teaching unbearable. Working in Manhattan restaurants was far more appealing at the time than getting up at dawn to teach English grammar. Up until that point, my theater education was minimal—I had taken one course and seen a total of perhaps a dozen plays. It didn't really seem to be a viable career choice. MTC, lodged in the Old Bohemian Hall on New York's upper east side, had three spaces operating at the time: the Downstage where the American Premier of Athol Fugard's, *Statements After the Arrest Under the Immorality Act,* just opened; the Upstage had Fugard's, *Nongogo,* directed by Oz Scott and starring Mary Alice; and the Cabaret featured the world premiere of *Ain't Misbehavin'* with Nell Carter, Amelia MacQueen, and Andre DeShields, among others. The bar was rolled into a hand-cranked elevator that opened onto the first floor vestibule and served as intermission lobby for the two stages. It also served as elevator for the Cabaret's *Ain't Misbehavin'* cast, and I would transport them to their dressing rooms during the break. After that gig, I was hooked on theater. I proceeded to work in the box office, the marketing department, and then the press department, gaining my real theater schooling in the two-and-one-half year paid apprenticeship at Manhattan Theatre Club.

"From there I worked as the marketing and press director for Manhattan Punch Line, an independent publicist for a number of theater productions, communications director for Circle Repertory Company from 1985 to1991, and press representative for New York Theater workshop from 1988 to 1991.

"Today my day-to-day work varies from month to month. However, it always focuses on writing—memos, faxes, press releases, photo identifications, letters, etc. I maintain a large database press list that is constantly changed, updated, and targeted. One of my goals is to attempt to get daily news updates from clients about their projects, and collect news that can sometimes be turned into items. In addition, I hire photographs for production photo shoots and work closely with the managing directors for all theaters, taking my cues from them. When I have information in advance, I do long-lead planning and pitches. Another major responsibility is to handle all opening nights, inviting the press, creating the press kits, and meeting and greeting on the actual day. During the height of the season (October/November), all of this can translate to about sixty hours per week.

"What I enjoy the most is dealing with the artists and the media. I enjoy working with writers—playwrights as much as critics—and it gives me tremendous pleasure to bring a playwright's work to the attention of the media. I have been fortunate to work with some of the finest artists appearing onstage during the last twenty years, and I've also worked with a number of vital theater institutions responsible for keeping American theater moving forward. They include the Manhattan Theatre Club, Circle Repertory Company, New York Theatre Workshop, and currently, The Geffen Playhouse.

"Don't follow in my footsteps. Make your own way. There are no set rules, no set game plan. If you want to be an actor, designer, or director, you can go to Juilliard, Yale, or Northwestern University and receive some of the best training available. Academic programs are available in theater administration, and I'd recommend that you choose one that gives you a solid liberal arts/business education along with the theater background. But more than that, if you want to work in theater today, you just have to love it. It's that simple. Because when you love what you do, nothing is too much, and the learning never stops."

## FOR MORE INFORMATION

Contact the following companies for additional information about career possibilities in this field.

Columbia Artists Management
    165 West Fifty-Seventh Street
    New York, NY 10019
    Contact: Human Resources

International Creative Management
    40 West Fifty-Seventh Street
    New York, NY 10019
    Contact: Director of Personnel

International Management Group
    One Erieview Plaza, Suite 1300
    Cleveland, OH 44114
    Contact: Director of Human Resources

Though not a bargaining union, there is an association for personal managers called the Conference of Personal Managers that sets standards of conduct for personal managers.

Business managers who are accountants may belong to:

American Institute of Certified Public
    Accountants (AICPA)
    1211 Avenue of the Americas
    New York, NY 10036

Contact the following associations for more information.

Association of Theatrical Press
　　Agents and Managers, AFL-CIO
　　(ATPAM)
　　165 West Forty-Sixth Street
　　New York, NY 10036

Conference of Personal Managers
　　(National)
　　210 East Fifty-First Street
　　New York, NY 10019

Institute of Certified Financial
　　Planners (ICFP)
　　7600 East Eastman Avenue,
　　Suite 301
　　Denver, CO 80231

International Association of Financial
　　Planning (IAFP)
　　Two Concourse Parkway, Suite 800
　　Atlanta, GA 30328

International Theatrical Agencies
　　Association (ITAA)
　　c/o Hartland Talent Marketing
　　5775 Wayzetta Boulevard
　　Minneapolis, MN 55426

League of American Theaters
　　and Producers
　　226 West Forty-Seventh Street
　　New York, NY 10036

Music Distributors Association
　　38 West Twenty-First Street,
　　5th Floor
　　New York, NY 10010

National Association of Accountants
　　(NAA)
　　10 Paragon Drive
　　Montvale, NJ 07645

National Society of Public
　　Accountants (NSPA)
　　1010 North Fairfax Street
　　Alexandria, VA 22314

Professional Arts Management
　　Institute
　　110 Riverside Drive, Suite 4E
　　New York, NY 10024

Recording Industry Association
　　of America
　　1020 Nineteenth Street, NW
　　Washington, DC 20036

## CHAPTER 6

# TEACHING MUSIC AND ACTING

To teach a man how he may learn to grow independently, and for himself, is perhaps the greatest service that one man can do to another.

—Benjamin Jowett

The ancient philosophers, Plato and Aristotle, endorsed music as an important aspect of a good citizen's life. In many ancient civilizations, music was considered a vital social activity. In Greece, for instance, children were taught to sing and play lyres, flutes, and harps at an early age. Today's music educators follow in this path.

## TEACHING MUSIC

Did you have a teacher who inspired you to seek a path as a music educator? Often, people attribute their career goals, at least in part, to teachers who served as role models. Perhaps you can serve in this capacity for others who will become your students.

In the field of music, teaching is a career that allows individuals who are very knowledgeable about a particular instrument (including the voice) to share their appreciation and expertise with others.

### School Music Teacher

The ultimate goal for all music educators is to provide children with a love for and an interest in music. To this end, they plan musical programs, encourage children to participate, coordinate musical activities with other school functions, or perhaps oversee activities in the community at large.

Music teachers, in both public and private schools, may be responsible for teaching music appreciation, history, literature, and theory to students from kindergarten through high school. In addition, educators may organize and direct school orchestras, choral groups, and other school-related music activities.

In elementary schools, music teachers may be responsible for teaching music in one school or several schools in the district, meeting with students once or several times a week. In the early grades, teachers are expected to focus on rhythm. Often they use marching and clapping to establish interest in this area. At this level, simple instruments such as recorders and rhythm instruments are used. The teacher may bring in a guitar to share music and songs with the children.

Administrative duties may include purchasing instruments, equipment, books, and sheet music. Additional responsibilities include keeping the musical equipment in shape, preparing budgets for programs, writing lesson plans and objectives, and evaluating the programs and progress of the students. Teachers are always called upon to attend meetings, serve on committees, meet with parents, work with students who have individual needs, supervise extracurricular projects, and meet other obligations dictated by the principal or the school board.

Some music teachers may entertain at functions and write their own songs and try to market them.

## Independent Music Teacher/Private Instrument or Voice Teacher

Teachers who give private lessons and who are self-employed have more freedom to set up their teaching programs as they wish. They may prefer to work with one or several students at a time. Some individuals find a site from which to teach or may travel to pupils' homes or teach from their own residences.

Successful private teachers must be able to make the experience enjoyable and informative for the students, allowing them to build their skills and love for music in the process.

As a culminating activity, teachers often schedule recitals for family and friends. This provides an opportunity for the students to work toward a goal, display their musical talents and effort, and raise their self-esteem for a job well done.

Teaching may be done on a full-time basis or in conjunction with a full- or part-time music position (or other occupation). Those who decide to do this kind of work need to build a clientele to make it worthwhile. Teachers charge anywhere from $15 or more per lesson.

## College, University, or Conservatory Music Teacher

Assistant professors, associate professors, and professors serve as music educators in colleges, universities, or conservatories. They may be responsible for teaching general music, music theory, music history, or instrumental and/or vocal performance. Other possibilities include conducting choruses or orchestras and publishing articles relating to the field.

Educators employed by community colleges usually teach approximately eighteen hours per week while those at four-year colleges or universities usually teach approximately nine to twelve hours per week. Added to that are the typical responsibilities of all teachers: preparation time, meetings, school events, availability to students, serving on committees, grading papers and exams, and evaluating students' progress in general. Total working hours probably number in excess of forty-five hours per week.

Since both public and private schools employ music teachers, the possibility of employment exists at all schools at all levels—elementary, secondary, and college as well as at music conservatories. Opportunities also exist in adult education programs and private lessons.

Music educators work in a school setting where they may be assigned to an ordinary classroom or a music room equipped with specially designed acoustics that help the music teacher to define and enrich the sound of the children's voices. The specially designed room may have semicircular risers or platforms. Rehearsals for chorus, orchestra, or band ensembles will be held here and led by the music teacher also.

Substantial time may be spent in other places, such as an assembly hall when special musical productions are offered or out-of-doors if the teacher's specific responsibilities call for this.

While those teaching in public or private schools may maintain a fairly normal schedule, those who give private lessons may have more irregular hours because of the necessity of working within the schedules of busy students and adults.

## TEACHING THEATER

Theater teachers instruct or coach students in the techniques of acting, directing, playwriting, script analysis, and the history of theater. They help students acquire confidence, assurance, speaking skills, and timing. They encourage students in their work, direct rehearsals, and guide pupils in their roles. At the same time, they instruct students in backstage work including set design, production organization, set building, stage lighting and sound, properties, costuming, and makeup.

At the high school level, theater may be a part of English or language arts. On the other hand, many high schools today have separate theater departments. They may offer classes in acting, directing, theater history, stagecraft, makeup, playwriting, wardrobe, speech arts, and theater management.

In most schools and colleges, theater teachers and administrators produce or direct plays for school and public performance. They audition students by cold reading of plays or listening to prepared auditions in order to judge the pupil's potential. Theater teachers also stress the front-of-the-house or management duties of a stage show. Students learn publicity and promotion, programs, tickets, ushering, and business procedures.

In general, college teachers are specialists in one or two theater arts. They may work in acting, which focuses on scenes, study, improvisation, voice for the actor, classical acting, and audition techniques. They may teach technical skills such as set construction, properties, lighting, sound, costume construction, and makeup. Some teach the art of directing, playwriting, or both. Others teach stage production and arts administration.

Theater teachers may lead seminars and workshops or arrange trips to professional plays or plays at other schools. They may work on drama forms such as mime, improvisation, and reader's theater. Some produce children's theater, summer theater, or dinner theater.

College teachers may also do research and write articles and books. They may take on projects such as plays by students or young playwrights. Some develop programs that give theater experience to troubled children. Others work to present traveling street theater or community or regional theater productions.

School theater departments often give two or three full-length plays or musicals each year for the student body and the public. Theater teachers may guide students who give plays in local, regional, state, and national contests. School theater clubs may have ties to national groups.

Dramatic coaches work with actors in an attempt to improve their acting techniques. They conduct readings to evaluate actors' abilities and then instruct them on how to improve their performances. Areas of concern may be stage presence, character interpretation, voice projection, or dialect.

Theater teachers work in almost every city and town. Most full-time theater teachers, however, work in or near large cities. They teach in public and private schools, colleges, and universities. Some work in regional theater, community theater, children's theater, or other groups that present theater productions.

## TRAINING FOR MUSIC TEACHERS

All public school music teachers must achieve state certification, which can be met through a bachelor's degree in music education at an accredited college or university. It is possible to teach at some private schools without certification, although this is becoming more and more rare.

Typical courses at the undergraduate level include:

background for teaching music in elementary school
background for teaching music in high school
child development
conducting
chorus
educational psychology
group voice
form and analysis
orchestration
piano musicianship
public performance
student teaching

Some states may require a master's degree for those preparing to join the staffs of elementary or secondary schools. Teaching at a college or conservatory always requires at least a master's degree. Many demand a doctoral degree. In addition, most positions require previous teaching experience.

It is important for teachers at all levels to be capable of working well with people, have an aptitude for conveying an enthusiasm about music to others, and have the ability to teach others. You will need to be skilled in playing at least one instrument (preferably more), have good communication skills, be independent, have initiative, possess a good sense of humor, and be intelligent, patient, and flexible.

For teachers giving private music lessons, it is necessary to have extensive training or study on a particular instrument or instruments, usually piano plus another instrument. In addition, they must possess the skills necessary to teach someone else how to play an instrument or sing with greater proficiency. Personal qualities include patience, good communications skills, and a true love of music.

## TRAINING FOR THEATER TEACHERS

Most theater teachers who are employed at the college level graduate with either a master's or a doctoral degree in theater or visual and performing arts. Those who plan to teach at the high school level must take courses in teaching methods, along with studies in drama. Some states offer certification in theater arts.

More than fifteen hundred colleges and universities in the United States offer undergraduate and graduate degrees in dramatic arts. Studies may include techniques of acting; history of the theater; understanding lighting, scenery, and costumes; analyzing and creating roles; working with directing concepts and techniques; techniques in script study and rehearsal; and lab sessions to gain experience.

College students may major in acting, child drama, directing, playwriting, theater design, theater education, stage technology, or theater management. A part of the training includes staging and acting in plays. In order to obtain a Master of Arts degree, students take the curriculum prescribed by the university and produce a thesis.

To get a Master of Fine Arts degree, students take mandatory courses along with electives, and do a creative project. They also must pass tests, both oral and written. Doctoral candidates must take more course work, must pass more examinations, and must write a dissertation on some aspect of the theater.

## Certification and Unions

Theater teachers in public and private elementary or high schools need state certification. Certification demands a college degree, a stated number of credits in a major, and courses in teaching methods.

Many school teachers belong to a union. The two principal ones are the National Education Association of the United States and the American Federation of Teachers. These unions negotiate contract terms on pay, tenure, working conditions, and other issues. College and high school teachers can also join the National Association of Dramatic and Speech Arts.

High school teachers may join the Theatre Education Association, which works to support theater programs in the educational system and emphasizes the importance of theater arts in the learning process. The American Alliance for Theatre and Education consists of educators, artists, administrators, and others serving young people in professional and community youth theaters and theater educational programs.

The Association for Theatre in Higher Education is a group of fifteen hundred individuals and five hundred organizations that foster the interaction and exchange of information among those engaged in theater research, performance, scholarship, and crafts. The association sets standards of excellence for organizations and individuals concerned with postsecondary theater training, production, and scholarship.

## SALARIES FOR MUSIC TEACHERS

Typical earnings for educators are listed below:

public school—$18,000 to $50,000
private school—$16,000 to $35,000
individual lessons—$10 to $30 per hour ($12,000 to $30,000+ per year)
conservatory—$25,000 to $70,000
college/university
    instructor—$25,000 to $37,000
        (nine to twelve teaching hours)
    assistant professor (Ph.D. level)—$35,000 to $50,000
        (nine to twelve teaching hours)
    associate professor (Ph.D. level)—$50,000 to $60,000
        (six to nine teaching hours plus supervision of doctoral students)

full professor (Ph.D. level)—$60,000 to $80,000
(three to six teaching hours plus supervision of doctoral students
and publication required)

Usually benefits for teachers are good and job security (after establishing tenure) is assured.

Typical benefits include:

hospitalization and other medical coverage
dental coverage
paid vacations
paid holidays
bonuses
life insurance
disability insurance
401 K or other financial vehicle
tuition reimbursement

## SALARIES FOR THEATER TEACHERS

In general, high school teachers are paid on a nine-month or ten-month contract. Yearly pay may range from a starting salary of about $20,000 to $40,000 after ten years of experience. Pay varies with the size of the city or town, the region of the country, and the number of years on the job. In most schools, where theater is an elective or extracurricular activity, teachers get a set amount along with their regular salary for leading the theater club or group and directing productions. This amount is generally between $2,000 and $5,000 per year.

The earnings of college theater teachers depends on their faculty rank. According to a recent report from the National Association of Colleges and Employers (formerly the College Placement Council), a graduate with a bachelor's degree in visual and performing arts received beginning offers averaging $18,541 per year. The College and University Personnel Association reported the average earnings for all faculty teaching visual and performing arts in four-year institutions at $41,152 in public universities and colleges and $38,733 in private institutions. Salaries ranged from $25,848 for instructors to $79,500 for professors. A report in the *College Planning Quarterly* lists $26,000 as the starting salary for graduates with a bachelor's degree in theater arts. Fringe benefits for teachers usually include health insurance and pension plans.

## CAREER OUTLOOK FOR MUSIC TEACHERS

Opportunities for music educators continue to increase as the popularity of music is spurred by new media techniques. On the other hand, when there are educational cutbacks, the music departments may be among the first to be affected. Positions at the college, university, and conservatory levels are not easy to come by, and competition for available positions is very stiff.

Prospects are always good for talented teachers who wish to give private, semiprivate, or group lessons. Word of mouth travels fast once someone is happy with their instructor or their child's instructor.

## CAREER OUTLOOK FOR THEATER TEACHERS

Although the demand for live theater today is not strong enough to support the many who seek to enter the field, countless individuals sign up to study theater in high school or college. These hopefuls create a demand for theater curricula and theater teachers.

The employment of college and university faculty as a whole is expected to increase through the year 2005. Many openings will arise as faculty retirements increase from the late 1990s through 2005. However, reduced budgets have cut some jobs, and those seeking work as theater teachers will, in fact, still face stiff competition.

## JOB STRATEGIES

When just starting out, you could contact music and instrument shops in your area and elucidate your credentials. Ask if they would be willing to recommend you to individuals seeking lessons. Have business cards made up that can be passed out at the retail establishments. Also contact public and private schools and religious organizations in your neighborhood to establish your credentials with them. Best targets for jobs would be large cities and metropolitan areas with enough people to warrant several private teachers.

*Be aware of teacher certification requirements.* Make sure you are aware of all teacher certification requirements in your state so there are no unpleasant surprises. Attend a school that will give you the credentials you need for state certification. Some positions will require that you get a master's degree and/or take a proficiency exam.

*Take advantage of school placement services and approach school systems directly.* Work through your school's placement service and also approach school systems directly. Have your resume and cover letter ready. (Include your philosophy of music or theater education. Tell why you think these subject areas are important.) If they have no openings now, ask them to keep your credentials on file in case an opening occurs. Summer sessions may provide a good opportunity for you to get your foot in the door.

*Check newspapers, employment agencies, and the Internet.* Other avenues for finding jobs include reading the weekly want ads (available at most libraries), investigating employment agencies (some specialize in working with teachers), and surfing on the Internet. The World Wide Web has a vast number of areas that offer career advice and provide information about job openings and further contacts.

*Go to job fairs.* Job fairs that focus on educational possibilities may provide you with knowledge of openings or contacts for future positions.

## Special Contacts for Positions at Higher Levels of Education

Those who seek positions at institutions of higher learning (and who have earned a Ph.D.) will probably need to prepare a curriculum vitae (CV) instead of or in addition to a resume. This vehicle stresses your interests, experience, publications, and achievements in research. A good resource to help you prepare this is VGM Career Horizon's, *How to Prepare Your Curriculum Vitae.*

For positions at the college, university, or conservatory level, you may obtain a list of openings called the Music Faculty List, provided by the College Music Society (CMS) and the American Musicological Society (AMS) The list is available to members. The Chronicle of Higher Education also publishes a weekly newspaper that features a list of faculty positions available in colleges and universities. In addition, you should approach institutions of higher learning directly.

## Special Resources

*Peterson's Guide to Independent Secondary Schools* and the *Handbook of Private Schools* are two excellent resources. They are published by Porter Sargent Publishers of Boston. Another helpful resource is *Independent School,* a publication of the Journal of the National Association of Independent Schools; it is published three times yearly. Other resources include *Current Jobs for Graduates in Education, Job Hunter, Community Jobs, Current Jobs for Graduates,* and *Patterson's American Education* and *Patterson's Elementary Education* published by Educational Directories.

## PROFILES

### Meet Chris Goeke

Chris Goeke is an assistant professor of voice at Southeast Missouri State University in Cape Girardeau, Missouri. Her background includes a B.A. degree in music and an M.A./D.M.A in voice performance and pedagogy. Added to that are private coaching with voice teachers and coaches in New York City, and classes and workshop performances in New York City.

"Coming from a musical family, I have always been involved with music in some way," says Goeke. "I started by playing trumpet in junior high school. In high school, I started performing in summer musicals. This was really important because I then began identifying myself as a performer. During college I worked as a shop assistant in the opera department. When I was working on my master's degree, I was an assistant voice teacher. During and after my formal education, I gained experience in a whole range of performing activities, including a large amount of church and synagogue work (primarily on weekends), considerable chorus work, and singing small parts and participating in concerts. In 1990 I was an adjunct professor at Grinnell College and a teaching assistant at the University of Iowa.

"In my present position, a doctoral degree in voice is required. Also necessary are skills in singing; a voice that people find pleasing; teaching experience; good organizational and planning skills; the ability to communicate effectively one-on-one; good piano skills (preferably at least at the intermediate level); awareness of musical styles such as opera, art songs, and musical theater; and the ability to speak another language. Additionally, you must enjoy researching music, be sensitive to various personalities, and understand voice development over the course of four years.

"I usually work from about 8:15 A.M. until about 5:00 P.M.," Goeke says. "A week's work usually amounts to about fifty hours, with hours devoted in the evenings and at least one day every weekend. Early mornings are generally spent with preparatory work and/or planning. I have one or two hours of classroom instruction along with three hours of individual instruction. Time is also spent in rehearsals for myself or a school activity. And, of course, no day would be complete without a meeting or two. Evening hours are filled with grading, planning, rehearsals, attending concerts, etc. When it comes time to prepare for a show, I work with the orchestra and theater department and things really get busy!

"I have my own office, which has a piano/desk and nice audio, video, and stereo equipment. This resulted from a grant I received for researching how audio and video equipment play a role in voice lessons. The work office is relaxed and congenial and, with minimal supervision, I am free to do what I feel is needed. However, I am evaluated twice a year by the faculty and at the end of every course by the students.

"I like the freedom the job offers and the fact that I am working in a field that I enjoy," stresses Goeke. "I like being creative. What I like least are the hours, which include evenings and weekends.

"To others who are considering getting into this field, I would say to make sure that wherever you decide to go to school, you'll be able to communicate and learn from your teacher. You need to have good one-on-one voice training. Your decision as to whom you will train with will affect your musical style and teaching ability in the years to come. I also would stress that professional experience is really helpful. Don't get all your training in a formal setting. By getting out there, you will gain more practical and beneficial experience. The more and varied the experience, the better. This will provide you with a good solid foundation for the future.

"Teaching and performing are very gratifying. Watching your students transform as people and performers over the course of years is also very rewarding. People enter into music careers for different reasons; some for money, experience, or because they truly enjoy it. It's a difficult business to be in unless you really want it. You have to view it as something worth sticking with. And if you want to achieve any measure of success, you'll have to pay your dues and work your way up the ladder."

## Meet Rick Davis

Rick Davis is the artistic director of the Theater of the First Amendment and an associate professor of theater at the Institute of the Arts at George Mason University in Fairfax, Virginia. His education includes a Bachelor of Arts degree in theater and drama from Lawrence University in Appleton, Wisconsin, and a Master's of Fine Arts in dramaturgy, dramatic literature, and criticism from the Yale School of Drama.

"I came to Theater of the First Amendment in 1991 directly from a six-season stint at Center Stage in Baltimore, where I began as a resident dramaturg and ended up as an associate artistic director," Davis says. "I was attracted to the program here at George Mason University because it combines a professional, Equity resident company with a liberal-arts undergraduate theater program, an experiment I thought well worth undertaking, and quite a rare if not a unique combination. I was also at a point in my career (about eight years out of graduate school with a variety of experiences under my belt both in the professional theater and in academia) where I wanted to try my hand at running a theater and a theater program. TFA and GMU offered the chance to do both in a supportive environment.

"For as long as I can remember—or, to be strictly accurate, once I stopped wanting to be a mad scientist—I wanted to work on plays: almost anything to do with plays, from writing to designing to directing to (occasionally and not too successfully) acting in them. My formal involvement in theater began on the community level when I was about ten or so, running a light board. I think it is significant that my first 'job' was on a production of *A Midsummer Night's Dream,* so that the imprint on my impressionable young mind was that a play should include poetry, music, dance, mythology, fantasy, and miraculous resolutions. I think I continue to look for all of those things today, in part with my ten-year-old eyes.

"In college I tried very hard to pretend that I wasn't going to major in theater, as a way of testing my level of commitment to it. The tests always resolved themselves in favor of theatrical work, though, so the early pattern was increasingly confirmed. Every summer, from age eighteen on, I found some way to earn a little money doing plays—summer stock technical work, some directing, some lighting design, some janitorial work (in a theater!)—whatever would fill the summer with drama and pay for at least some of the associated expenses. Four summers of repertory stock in Colorado, during the transition defined by finishing college and starting grad school, really proved to me that I wanted to make this a life's career.

"In graduate school, several of us banded together to start a theater that would commence operations literally days after our graduation. We raised money, contributed what little we could, did publicity, scouted spaces, chose plays and artists and staff, and launched the American Ibsen Theater in Pittsburgh in the summer of 1983. We had three very interesting, critically successful, and challenging seasons before some of our management naïveté caught up with us and we ran out of money. But I would not trade the experience of being in on the founding of a theater for anything. The level of commitment it requires is total, and the sense of emotional and artistic investment is profound. It shapes you forever.

"I was extremely fortunate to be employed during this period as a faculty member at Washington College, a lovely small school on Maryland's eastern shore. That job provided a secure, if modest, financial base, a home to return to, and an intellectually and artistically stimulating environment in which to try out ideas—and it is the place where I learned how to teach. When the Ibsen Theater folded, Washington College was generous enough to allow me to take a year-round position at Center Stage in Baltimore and craft a schedule that, for a couple of years anyway, was sustainable.

"Center Stage was an immersion in the world of the large, well-funded, and well-managed institutional theater. What a difference from the Ibsen Theater! Center Stage was and is artistically driven, but it has sophisticated, mature leadership that recognizes how difficult it can be to be a 'grown-up' and maintain a theater career. They've taken steps to make sure that the things that drive people away from the business once they reach their thirties— burnout, low pay, poor benefits, a frenzied atmosphere—are brought under control to the largest extent possible. It was great for me to be a part of that for long enough to appreciate how it's done, and how important it is.

"Since I both direct a company and teach, there's a built-in schizophrenia in my job that I cherish: Not that my attention span is unusually short, but I crave variety and change, and they come with the territory here. There is no typical day, but over the last couple of days this summer I've read a play for consideration for the season after next; interviewed a costume designer; spoken long-distance to the composer of our upcoming production about the vocal range of one of the parts and discussed with the director what effect that will have on casting; talked to the set designer of the next play I'm directing; had four university committee meetings ranging from curriculum planning to marketing; proofread a brochure; worked on a press release; and given a lecture. All of that goes on pretty much all the time, and this is our quiet season! Once the school year and the theater season start, add directing, producing, and teaching to the list. It is busy, yes, but we strive to create an unhurried atmosphere in our work that is susceptible to humor, irony, and the recognition of those moments when enough is enough. In general, I'd say that I look forward to coming to work every day.

"I thrive on the variety of challenges that come my way in any given week. I love directing plays and operas above all, and this job allows me to do that several times a year (and, crucially, allows me off campus opportunities when they come about). I love to teach, and I find that teaching reinforces theater work and vice versa. I like the interactions among students, colleagues, and artists that a place like this tends to foster. I like hearing from alumni who are out there doing what they want to do.

"In any institution, but especially in larger-sized academic institutions, there are bureaucracies, traditions, procedures, and other ways of making it difficult to do one's work quickly and sensibly. In academia, there is also an unnatural enthusiasm for committees. And there is tenure. Overall, a university can be a supportive and exciting place to work if you keep your eye on what works and don't get consumed by what doesn't. That is true in theaters as well.

"Realize that no scrap of experience or knowledge is ever wasted when one is pursuing a life in the theater. Be hungry for as much of both as you can handle. Read widely, listen to music (all kinds), look at lots of pictures, read the newspaper every single day. Cultivate collaborators in whom you have confidence and for whom you have enthusiasm. Have at least one thing you do outside the theater that is important and stimulating to you. Etymologize the word 'liberal' as in 'liberal arts,' and recognize that it's not exactly what most people think it is. Then pursue it."

## Meet Harris D. Smith

Harris D. Smith is an assistant professor of theatre arts at Central Washington University in Ellensburg, Washington. He earned a Bachelor of

Arts degree in theatre arts from Montana State University in Bozeman and a Master of Fine Arts degree in theatre arts (acting emphasis) from the University of Washington, Seattle (whose graduate department is currently ranked number four in the country by *Newsweek* magazine). He is also certified by the Society of American Fight Directors (SAFD) as an actor/combatant in stage combat. He was trained by David Boushey (fight master and founder of the SAFD at the University of Washington and one of the few fight masters certified in both Britain and America), and is a member of the United Stuntmen's Association, Screen Actors Guild, and Actors' Equity Association.

His professional work as an actor includes: *Amazing Grace and Chuck, Runaway Train,* and *Chips the War Dog* (films), and *Pandora's Clock* (television miniseries) and as an actor/stuntman on the *X-Files* interactive CD ROM.

"The fortunate thing about teaching and acting is that Shakespeare festivals and summer stock happen during the summer," Smith says, "so I'm able to do a little of that, too. One of my more enjoyable roles was playing Tybalt (in *Romeo and Juliet*) at the Utah Shakespearean Festival.

"I started teaching in 1993 at the State University of New York (SUNY) at Albany," says Harris. "I went into graduate school planning to become a university professor. After several years of full-time professional acting work, I applied for the position at Central. My professional experience includes working with the Sacramento Theatre Company; A Contemporary Theatre (ACT) (Seattle, Washington); Seattle Children's Theatre; and the St. Louis (Missouri) Black Repertory.

"I was attracted to the art of creating illusion," he says. "I feel that when drama is done well—in whatever genre—it can be very powerful, moving, even dangerous—dangerous not just physically but politically, morally, and emotionally. I get the most enjoyment out of seeing my students learn the skills needed to effectively create illusion.

"After teaching acting for a time, I found that I have a gift for sharing and teaching the art of illusion, particularly in stage combat. As a college football player, I understood the dangers of full contact in what some consider to be a violent sport. On stage, I have the chance to create that illusion of danger without bodily harm. I find this to be much more rewarding, and a lot healthier.

"Overall, I would say my athletic background and the aspect of sports as entertainment had the greatest influence on me. Besides, I love to perform.

"Between teaching and advising my students, service on departmental and university committees, and a wife and three children, I keep quite busy during the year. I spend the majority of my day in the classroom. Generally I teach at least two classes per day along with assisting on other department projects (including some acting in theatrical productions) that are going on throughout the year.

"Up to a sixty-hour workweek is typical, especially when I'm working on a production. Central's theater department is constantly growing, and with growth comes change and adjustment. This can be particularly challenging—but gratifying—when what you do enhances the education of many students.

"I'm lucky to be working with some of the most gifted colleagues in my profession, which helps me to be even more effective in the classroom and on the collegiate stage. We share a common goal: to produce talented, well-rounded students in the arts.

"To me, teaching is one of the greatest jobs you can have. What I enjoy most is working with the students and pushing them to achieve beyond what they thought was possible. For example, about five weeks into one of my classes, I require my students to perform a singing exercise. They may have to sing a capella. When they read the syllabus the first day of class, I know they see that exercise and think 'no way.' After the performances, they are generally patting each other on the back and discussing how great and moving the songs were. It's so rewarding to see them take risks and achieve their goals. You can't put a price on that.

"I ask my students to try to picture Michael Jordan with his muscles all tensed up and nervous, trying to move around the basketball court floor. If he were, he wouldn't be able to be spontaneous and create all the moves he does. He just free-flows, and actors have to do the same thing.

"My least favorite tasks include paperwork, grading, and other administrative tasks. I find grading to be particularly difficult. How do you grade someone on their life experiences, or lack thereof?

"I would encourage potential theater educators to pace yourselves. Students will suck up everything you have to offer, which is great. But, you need to have a portion of yourself left over to bring home at night to give to your family, who love you more than anyone else. And, what you have for them must be genuine, for they know better than anyone when you're acting."

## Meet Steve Schrum

Steve Schrum is a lecturer at Penn State University at Hazleton, Pennsylvania. He earned his Bachelor of Arts degree in theater from Temple University in Philadelphia, his Master of Arts from Ohio State University in Columbus, and his A.B.D in directing from the University of California in Berkeley.

"In high school I became interested in film and started making them with super 8 (film)," says Schrum. "When I went to college as a communications major, I wanted to become a television/video director, but I also did radio and theater, too. Somewhere along the line, I decided that I liked working in theater better. Part of it was working with actors over a longer period of time, rather than a quickie rehearsal before putting someone in front of a camera. Also, I preferred the live aspect of the performance, getting immediate feedback from the audience and using that to fuel the performance. As the years continue, I prefer the whole idea of collaboration with actors and designers who can take my basic ideas and flesh them out to make more of them than any of us working alone could have created.

"I am always busy, since teaching always requires something—preparation for class, upgrading my presentations (in which I use considerable multimedia), getting ready for rehearsals. And the workload varies from busy to extremely busy during the semester. The busiest time is prior to production, since I am generally working full-time on getting the show ready while still teaching class.

"A typical day starts with checking e-mail from students (I have them turn in assignments via e-mail), preparing for class (which is a quick rehearsal of the day's events), and teaching. In the evening, I have rehearsals for the productions. On days that I don't teach, I am either doing planning for the show, working on the software for my next class presentation, or doing any of the many outside projects that I juggle constantly.

"Hours a week vary, but I often put in ten hours a day, five days a week on average, doing work-related things—and that's for a part-time, underpaid lecturer.

"What I like most about my work is that, first of all, I am working and am doing not only what I was trained to do but what I enjoy most—directing and teaching (the latter also being an opportunity for performing for me). I also have a chance to direct whatever I want, which is great, and I have a measure of freedom to develop projects that bring computers and theater together. The university provides me with the hardware and software needed to do what I like to do. The things I like the least are my part-time salary (per credit and not really a salary) and the fact that I work hard on the productions and yet many people don't bother coming to the shows. However, the things I like the most outweigh the negatives.

"I would advise that candidates for this career do as much production work as you can in as many areas as you can to get as much practical experience as possible. For the academics, read as many plays as possible and try to make connections between everything. And don't let the semester-sized lumps—as someone once called them—of theater history be all you know. Do as much extra reading as possible to provide yourself with as extensive and comprehensive a knowledge of theater as possible."

## FOR MORE INFORMATION

American Federation of Teachers
(AFT)
555 New Jersey Avenue, NW
Washington, DC 20001

American Federation of Teachers of
the United States and Canada
1501 Broadway, Suite 600
New York, NY 10036

American Musicological Society
201 South Thirty-Fourth Street
University of Pennsylvania
Philadelphia, PA 19104

College Band Directors National
Association
Box 8028
University of Texas
Austin, TX 78713

College Music Society
202 West Spruce
Missoula, MT 59802

Music Educators National Conference
1806 Robert Fulton Drive
Reston, VA 22091

Music Teacher National Association
617 Vine Street, Suite 505
Cincinnati, OH 45202

National Association of College Wind
and Percussion Instructors
(NACWPI)
Divison of Fine Arts
Northeast Missouri State
University
Kirksville, MO 63501

National Association of Schools of
Music
11250 Roger Bacon Drive, Suite 21
Reston, VA 22091

Society for Music Teacher Education
1806 Robert Fulton Drive
Reston, VA 22091

## Professional Associations—Theater

American Alliance for Theatre and
  Education
Arizona State University
Theatre Department
Box 873411
Tempe, AZ 85287

American Federal of Teachers
555 New Jersey Avenue, NW
Washington, DC 20001

American Theatre Works, Inc.
  Theatre Directories
  P.O. Box 519
  Dorset, VT 05251

Association for Theatre in Higher
    Education
  c/o Theatre Service
  200 North Michigan Avenue,
    Suite 300
  Chicago, IL 60601

National Association of Dramatic and
    Speech Arts
  208 Cherokee Drive
  Blacksburg, VA 24060

National Association of Schools
    of Theatre
  11250 Roger Bacon Drive, Suite 21
  Reston, VA 22090

National Education Association of the
    United States
  1201 Sixteenth Street, NW
  Washington, DC 20036

Theatre Communications Group
    (TCG)
  355 Lexington Avenue
  New York, NY 10017

Theatre Education Association
  3368 Central Parkway
  Cincinnati, OH 45225

## CHAPTER 7

# CAREERS IN WRITING

If you want to change the world, pick up your pen.
—Martin Luther

Writers are creative individuals who can "invent" something out of nothing. To some, the blank page is too daunting to approach; to others it is an everyday task and a welcome, invigorating challenge. Composers, songwriters, playwrights, and screenwriters are, in a very real sense, etching our culture into history and recording it for all generations to come.

## COMPOSER

Composers write music for both instrumentals and vocals in a variety of forms: popular music, classical music, rhythm and blues tunes, symphonies, ballets, operas, radio or television commercials, theme music, background music, sonatas, Broadway music, jazz, country, and many others.

For instance, composers may be hired to write the music for theatrical musical productions or operas. As is the case with any musical production, composers usually work from a script after conferring with the writers, producers, and directors of the show to gain a better understanding and feeling for what the work is all about.

Songs must always fit in with a play's theme. All of the specifications that must be met make this profession a difficult one, especially since all of the people involved must like what the composer has created. If this is not the case, the composer must begin all over again.

Geographically, it is possible to write songs in any area of the country, actually any area of the world. However, staff positions with producers, recording groups, or recording companies are more easily secured in cities like Los Angeles, New York, or Nashville, Tennessee.

For talented composers who are looking to begin a career writing for musical productions, prospects exist in smaller theaters and production companies. Otherwise, you must team up with someone who will be willing to finance the project.

Once composers have established a reputation, they may be approached by producers to write the music for their project. Composers who have gotten good reviews will be offered additional projects.

## SONGWRITER

Songwriters may focus on writing melodies, lyrics, or both. Their songs may be designed to be sung by performers at concerts or on CDs; as part of the music for plays, television, films; or even as radio or television jingles. Songwriters may operate alone or develop a partnership (collaboration) working with another music professional.

There are two basic approaches to writing music. Most songwriters write at specific times during the day or night, establishing a regular routine just as everyone in any profession does. Some songwriters may wait for inspiration and write when the mood or the spirit moves them to write. But this is a risky approach to this profession, especially if you are interested in making a living at it.

Once songs are written, songwriters must officially copyright them through specific governmental agencies. There is another procedure in which the songwriter places a finished piece of music in a self-addressed envelope, sends it to himself or herself via certified registered mail, and keeps it intact without opening it. Most people in the business believe that copyrighting through official channels is much safer.

Songwriters must not only write songs, they must learn to be effective at marketing them. Nothing is gained if that is not accomplished because there can be no "hit" if the song is never heard.

In order to get attention for a song, the songwriter will make up demos and send them to people who might be in a position to further the song's potential. Before doing this, however, it's a good idea to mail a letter that highlights its features and piques the reader's interest. If successful, the song may be accepted by a recording group, music publisher, or some other individual associated with the music business who can promote it.

## ARRANGER

Arrangers are faced with the task of changing an existing piece of music to create new harmonies and alter and improve its rhythms. Arranging may be performed for any musical instrument. Proficient arrangers will rework a song with current trends in mind to try to turn it into a hit. They may work for music services like Muzak or for music publishers, for television, or for the motion picture industry. Sometimes, established musicians move on to become arrangers, often working as freelance professionals.

## PLAYWRIGHT

Playwrights write original plays such as tragedies, comedies, or dramas or adapt themes from fictional, historical, or narrative sources for dramatic presentation. Sometimes an individual writes a play and then attempts to locate a producer to finance it and put it into production. In other cases, a producer may have an idea and retain a playwright to develop the script.

In order for the playwright to write a script, he or she first develops an idea for a story. The individual must then tell the story. There are many areas that must be considered. Will it be a comedy, mystery, thriller, or musical? Who will the characters be? What will they be like? What will the setting be? How will the story be told? What conflicts will the characters be involved in? What will the resolutions be? What will the climax of the play be? How will it end?

When a playwright creates a story, it must be written in a specific form for the theater. The script must be written in dialogue. Generally, a script indicates the dialogue that a character is supposed to speak. The lines are next to or under the individual character's name. The playwright also must include settings of scenes, settings' descriptions, and movements that a particular character must make.

Since playwrights often work by themselves, their day-to-day existence can become quite lonely. However, most prominent playwrights feel that seeing their ideas, stories, and innermost thoughts presented for all to see is enough to keep them going through the preliminary stages of creating something new.

There are more opportunities in this field in culturally active cities. An aspiring playwright can look for a job as a playwright-in-residence at a repertory, community, or school theater. Individuals also might submit their scripts to producers who have not yet made a name for themselves, but also are trying to break into the business. Other possibilities include community theaters, college theaters, and experimental theaters. These kinds of groups often are looking for new plays to present.

## SCREENWRITER

Writing screenplays for movies incorporates a little bit of theater and a little bit of television. You go about writing for movies the same way as you do for television, except that you can send your scripts to independent producers and to production companies. But there are film-writing courses, both in colleges and in other educational facilities, that will help you learn the craft of writing for film.

A screenwriter writes scripts designed for entertainment, education, training, sales, and films. Themes may be chosen by the screenwriters themselves or by a producer or director. Every show or movie you see is written by someone in the form of a script.

If you have already written a script, you might want to send it to an agent. Before doing so, you would need to compose a cover letter telling him or her that you are interested in writing for television and would like representation. Indicate that you are enclosing a sample script. If the agent is interested in you, he or she will try to secure writing positions for you on various shows. To deal with television and motion picture people, you usually need an agent.

## DRAMA (OR THEATER) CRITIC

Critics, in general, can seriously affect whether or not a play or other comedy or dramatic event will meet with real success, both financial and otherwise. Drama critics are assigned the responsibility of viewing plays and writing their opinions of the performances.

## ON THE JOB

Composers and arrangers often do much of their work as a solitary endeavor. Usually the work place is one's home or studio.

Since those who engage in this kind of work must often juggle a number of projects all at one time, they may be required to work days, evenings, weekends, and even holidays if deadlines must be met. In order to accomplish this, a great deal of discipline and planning are required and stress must be overcome.

Freelance screenwriters or playwrights can choose when and where to write. However, if you are lucky enough to find work and do not reside in Hollywood or New York City, you may need to travel before and after the production. Relocation is even a possibility.

Because there are also long periods of inactivity while trying to get projects chosen by studio executives or directors, most screenwriters have a second job in order to meet living expenses.

## TRAINING FOR COMPOSERS, SONGWRITERS, AND ARRANGERS

Though no formal education may be required to become a songwriter, composer, or arranger, a great deal of knowledge, expertise, and musical ability are required to be successful in these careers. Those interested in doing this kind of work often attend colleges, universities, or conservatories and major in music and/or theater arts. Studying music theory, orchestration, and harmony are valuable. Many times songwriters, composers, and arrangers began musical training at an early age and are proficient on at least one instrument.

To build toward a career as a composer, experts advise that you become familiar with all kinds of productions involving music, listen to a variety of Broadway musicals and operas, write for school and/or local productions, find a related internship (also check with local production companies to see if they provide any kind of workshops or other training vehicles), and work in summer stock or regional theater productions. Experience in writing poetry also may come in handy.

Music conferences, workshops, and the like also will increase an individual's expertise in composing and arranging. Both experience and contacts are gained when arranging music for others or through working as a copyist (one who does transcribing). Other possibilities include playing an instrument in a professional arena such as in a band or symphony or applying for a grant from the National Endowment of the Arts (NEA).

On a personal level, composers need to be creative, disciplined, musically talented, persistent, and patient. Also required are sufficient business acumen, worthwhile music contacts, knowledge of instruments, and adaptability. Good timing and a measure of good luck are also pluses.

## TRAINING FOR PLAYWRIGHTS, SCREENWRITERS, AND CRITICS

While college will not guarantee success to a playwright, it is often useful. Colleges offering majors in theater, theater arts, scriptwriting, or acting often have programs where aspiring playwrights can have their plays worked on, further developed, and produced at the school. This offers playwrights opportunities and experiences others might not have.

Seminars, courses, and workshops in all facets of writing, including scriptwriting as well as stage, theater, and acting, will be helpful in honing skills.

The more writing experience a playwright can garner, the better. Writing skills and techniques need to be polished. Playwrights should have an excellent command of the English language and an ability to write dialogue effectively. They need to be creative and exciting and have the ability to bring stories to life. These also could be in the form of short stories, novels, or articles in magazines and newspapers. Entering writing contests (particularly playwriting contests) is an excellent way of getting noticed. Often these contests offer a staged reading or full production as the prize.

Playwrights must also be capable of marketing their plays. Once they are finished, it's wise to have them bound and copyrighted at the Copyright Office of the Library of Congress.

There are no set educational requirements for screenwriters. A college degree is desirable, especially one in theater or liberal arts that exposes the students to a wide range of subjects. Screenwriters must be able to create believable characters and build a story. They must possess a range of technical skills such as writing dialogue, creating plots, and doing research. Word processing and computer skills also are necessary.

Screenwriters must be persistent, patient, imaginative, creative, and skilled in negotiation techniques. They also must have the ability to tell a good story and possess expertise in verbal and written communications.

Newspapers, magazines, web sites, and other forms of communication may employ drama critics. To begin, contact a local publication and ask if you can review a dramatic event (even if you don't get paid for it). You need to begin to build clips (published articles). This way you may be able to work your way up to paid assignments, larger newspapers or magazines, or other types of publications.

Don't expect this to be a nine-to-five job. Drama critics may work evening and weekend hours and be faced with difficult deadlines.

## SALARIES FOR COMPOSERS, SONGWRITERS, AND ARRANGERS

Since most composers and arrangers are self-employed, it is important to factor in the reality that they must provide their own benefits, including health insurance, vacation time, and pension. They also must absorb expenses such as copying fees, traveling costs, mailings, and organizational dues that can amount to several thousand dollars per year.

For established composers, payments or royalties often are earned every time their work is performed or published. Composers share with producers, who receive one-half of performance royalties.

Though earnings will vary, the following list provides a range of figures:

film score—up to $30,000
half-hour television show—up to $2,500
television movie—$12,000 to $15,000
television four-hour miniseries—up to $30,000
lyricist per song—up to $8,000

Yearly salaries will depend on a number of factors: how many songs are published or sold, how popular the song is, how many times it is played, and the agreement reached for each tune. As is the case with books, songs may be sold for one flat fee or be subject to royalties for the publisher and/or writer. If songs are the result of collaborations, the total earnings will be split evenly between the two parties involved. Very successful songwriters may make $500,000 to $1,000,000 per year. However, it is also quite conceivable to earn only $1,000 to $8,000.

## SALARIES FOR PLAYWRIGHTS, SCREENWRITERS, AND CRITICS

There are a number of ways for a playwright to earn money. Individuals can write a script and then sell it outright for an agreed-upon sum of money. They also might accept what is known as an option payment on a script. An option gives a producer the rights to the script for a specific period of time. During this period, the producer attempts to locate financing. If financing is obtained, the producer will fine tune the negotiations for the rights. Each time the script is performed, the playwright will then receive a royalty. This is similar to the way songwriters are paid for tunes they have written. Some playwrights have never earned a penny for their work, and others have earned millions over a period of many years.

Earnings for screenwriters depend on contract negotiations. Some writers receive a percentage of box office receipts. Here are some average figures for those in the field:

    beginning screenplay writer with treatment—$54,000
    established screenplay writer—$600,000
    two-hour television movie script—$47,000
    staff writers (for a guaranteed number of weeks)—$4,860 per week

Though earnings will vary according to the location of the job, the following represent average salaries for critics:

    local newspaper, writing reviews (no experience)—$15,000 minimum
       per year
    local newspaper, with experience—$20,000 to $25,000 per year
    major publication—$17,500 to $100,000 per year

## CAREER OUTLOOK

Competition is so keen that the outlook for those interested in these careers is not very promising. However, with talent, patience, and perseverance, one can succeed.

Only a small percentage of playwrights are able to sustain themselves full-time in this career. However, there are a number of people who are able to get their plays produced by smaller, community theaters and are waiting for reviews to build a solid enough reputation to take them to writing off-Broadway plays and then Broadway plays. The competition in this area is fierce as it is for theater in general.

There is intense competition in the television and motion picture industries. As cable television expands, new opportunities may emerge. Television networks continue to need new episodes for long-running series. Demand should increase slightly in the next decade, but the number of screenwriters is growing at a faster rate. Writers also will find opportunities with advertising agencies, educational training, and training video production houses.

## PROFILES

### Meet Lisa Morton

Lisa Morton is a freelance screenwriter from North Hollywood, California. She attended film school at UCLA and San Diego State, but she left school to work in the film industry before receiving a degree.

When asked what attracted Lisa to the profession, she says, "Simple: I had no choice! Writing is the only thing I've ever wanted to do, and fortunately for me, it's what I do best.

"I actually started in the film industry as a special effects model maker, while writing one script after another on the side. After working in the industry for several years, I was able to use my contacts to sell my first script."

When she's not writing, Lisa enjoys working part-time in a used bookstore. "I've always worked in bookstores," she says. "If you don't love to read, you shouldn't become a writer. I love being around books and people, because writing can be pretty solitary. And it keeps me grounded!

"There is no typical day for me. Although I'm lucky enough to be employed as an animation writer on a fairly regular basis, there are usually weeks between script assignments. Then I work on my own scripts. When an assignment comes in, they usually need the script so quickly—five days is an average deadline for my half-hour animated scripts—that my life becomes about nothing but finishing that script. And then, of course, there are the meetings with producers and directors and development executives, and…I'd rather be writing, frankly!

"What I like most, of course, and what I sometimes still find hard to believe, is that I'm being paid to do the one thing in life I've always loved doing the most.

"Downsides? The wait time between jobs. Sometimes you wonder if there will even be a next job. Another downside for me is the business angle of being an independent contractor. Business is not my strong point.

"My advice is to write all the time. Study the good films. If you want a way to get rich quick, go be a stockbroker. If you have a hard time dealing with rejection, get over it or get out. Most importantly, do whatever you can to get into the industry, even if it means taking jobs that don't have anything to do with writing. You must develop your own contacts or you won't have a prayer of succeeding, no matter how talented you are."

## Meet Rick Rhodes

Rick Rhodes is an Emmy Award–winning composer and the president of Rhodes Communications, Inc., a music design company in California. He completed some college courses but says that his main experience comes from playing many instruments and performing in rock and roll bands in the seventies and eighties. His songs have been recorded by a multitude of artists including Patti Austin, Special EFX, Tiffany, Diane Schuur, Tom Scott, Bill Champlin, Richard Elliot, and many more. Rick also has written songs with Bobby Caldwell, Dave Koz, Chieli Minucci, Grant Geissman, Lorraine Feather, Don Grusin, Russ Freeman, David Pack, and many other notable artists and songwriters.

Rhodes currently composes music for television shows, interactive games, and production music libraries. He has won Emmys for the music he wrote for the television soap operas *Santa Barbara, Another World,* and *Guiding Light.* Other television credits include *Family Ties, Lifestyles of the Rich and Famous,* and *As the World Turns.* Film credits include *Mars Attacks, McHale's Navy,* and *True Lies.*

As a recording artist, Rhodes has released three CDs, *Now You See It, Indian Summer,* and *Deep in the Night,* which are available worldwide.

As a theatrical producer, his credits include *A Midsummer Night's Dream* at California Lutheran University and productions of Charles Dickens's, *A Christmas Carol* and *Cabaret.*

"When I was a kid, composing looked like a fun way to make a living," says Rhodes. "Besides, I didn't know how to do anything else.

"My big break was getting onto the show *Santa Barbara*. It paved the way for new opportunities and opened the door to a new world for me. I work three or four hours a day, three or four days a week. That's basically it.

"There are many more good sides to this type of work than bad sides; however, it can be nerve-racking when the work is sparse.

"I would advise those considering this career to learn as much about writing music as you possibly can. Try to apprentice (even with no money) with someone you look up to. Your break will come from that!"

### Meet Beverly Shields

Beverly Shields received her B.A. from Illinois Wesleyan University and an M.A.T. from the University of Illinois, and she is currently working on an M.F.A. in screenwriting at the American Film Institute in Los Angeles. Besides pursuing a screenwriting career, she also teaches at a private school and performs regularly as a Judy Garland look-alike.

"I got started doing look-alikes when someone referred me to an agent several years ago," says Shields. "As for screenwriting, I just wanted to begin to write plays of my own, so I looked into the training programs. I have always loved singing and acting, and especially making people happy.

"Teaching has had a profound bearing on my performing. It has helped me in facing a group of people and talking all day—often to those who would rather be at the beach!

"Directing the school theater productions taught me everything I needed to know about acting. It was incredible. It was there that I learned I wanted to help kids to be all that they can be. I decided to show them, so I am now performing too.

"My performance jobs are sporadic. A performance can be in various places and for various types of crowds. I never know exactly what to expect. The hardest thing about these jobs is the waiting in between to find out when and where the next gigs are going to occur. I haven't been able to separate myself from my teaching job because I need to pay the bills. Full-time singing and acting don't give that kind of security right off the bat.

"What I like most about my performance job is the joy I get from singing and the joy I get from seeing people in the audience smiling back at me. I also love the acting part, especially the comedy element. It is so great to know that people are enjoying my attempt to entertain them! There is no greater joy.

"The downside is the small contingency of negative critics who seek to undermine anyone who is trying to entertain others. It can be difficult when you are on the receiving end of insults or discouraging e-mails. But those things do happen. There are some unhappy people out there, and many of them are blocked artists who would have loved to become performers themselves, before they allowed someone else to suppress them. It is difficult not to let those people's insults discourage me. But what keeps me going when I'm confronted by that is realizing that those people weren't born that way; someone hurt them first and they became that way.

"My advice to others is to do what makes your heart sing and don't let any person, place, or thing discourage you. Work hard and pray hard. Go for the highest good in your work. Do things that have a positive, not negative, effect on the world. There is already way too much pain and suffering out there. Be gentle with yourself so that you can bring more gentleness into a world that is truly starving for it. Learn to forgive those who try to discourage and hurt you. Harboring resentment is like holding onto a hot rock; the longer you hold onto it, the more it burns you. Don't carry it! Also, be your own best friend, and always remember to take time to eat, sleep, and breathe!"

### Meet Kevin Devine

Kevin Devine of Boston is a songwriter, children's entertainer, and recording artist. He earned a Bachelor of Arts degree in English language and literature at the University of Michigan, Ann Arbor, in 1983 and was awarded the Hopwood Writing Award in the same year. His additional training includes twelve years of private piano studies, five years of private voice lessons, and guitar and theory classes and lessons.

"I started performing professionally in a rock band in high school and played in bands and solo piano in nightclubs and restaurants in college and after," says Devine. "The turning point came at age twenty-four, while working as a writer/researcher. I was offered a full-time position as bass player with rockabilly legend Sleepy LaBeef. After two weeks, he fired me. It was the best thing that could have happened to me—musically.

"I was told that I needed more practice. As a result, I got more serious about music and songwriting. A few years later, while working as a newspaper reporter (and playing music here and there), I began directing a senior citizens choral group in my town as a volunteer. One day, a pre-school teacher brought her class in to hear one of our choral concerts. Subsequently, she invited me to sing with the children in her class the next week. I balked, claiming my knowledge of children's music was quite limited. She persevered, I accepted, and the rest, for me, is history!

"Then and there I quit my reporting job and began singing at schools, writing children's songs, and producing children's albums. It's been almost ten years now, and it's been great—not without its bumpy stretches of road (that most self-employed individuals encounter) but overall very rewarding, interesting, fulfilling and fun! I get to write and sing songs all day, playing whatever instruments I choose and being silly along the way. And my audiences are wonderful. They love to sing along and make music together.

"I like working independently and I love music and children. After years of working with children and as a parent myself, I also appreciate the importance of positive role models for young children and the tremendous responsibility early childhood educators have in shaping the confidence and self-esteem of youngsters. It's also a job that taps into my creative energy and forces me to keep learning and writing new and better material.

"Being a newspaper reporter was great training for just about anything, I'd have to say. You learn to write well, work well with people (including being pushy when you have to!), and above all, you learn to live with rejection and setbacks. Not everyone calls you back, sources go south, editors shred your copy, and deadlines are deadlines. You learn to pick up the pieces and keep on keeping on. As a reporter, one also learns to perform research, a skill that comes in quite handy when trying to book and promote oneself as a 'product' in the entertainment market and when looking for new markets for songs and venues for performing.

"My typical days are frenzied, singing at twelve or so schools each week with small groups of twenty to thirty children plus two to three large shows of three hundred to five hundred children each week at libraries, malls, schools, parks, etc. I'm also busy writing new songs for television shows and for my own albums and other performers; fielding calls from prospective concert or songwriting clients; coordinating publicity (writing and sending press releases and photos to publicize upcoming concerts); fulfilling cassette orders; book keeping; paying bills; driving, driving, and more driving!; and prospecting for new business by researching television shows and festival, event, and library directories.

"I usually end up eating lunch at the wheel of my car. My office work (correspondence, contracts, etc.) is generally done in my home office after 9:00 P.M. I do some demo recording at home but complete finished work at studios. As for performing live, the great thing about working with children is that the venues are all smoke- and alcohol-free and I rarely have to work past 7:00 P.M. (The only exceptions are New Year's Eve and Halloween!)

"What I like most about my work is that I'm able to be what I really am—a singer, songwriter, entertainer, and people person. I instigate the kind of fun I enjoy, and I perform at the kinds of events I like to attend with my wife and son—family-oriented festivals, concerts, museums, and parks.

"What I like least is that as a self-employed musician, in order to make a living and own a home and have cars and some semblance of a middle-class life, I have to work all the time. I don't intend to work this hard forever, even though I love the work. I'm spending more time working as a songwriter because the royalties could afford me (eventually) more time off and thus time with my family.

"I would advise others considering this kind of work to play anywhere and everywhere they'll take you. Musicians need to play before live audiences if they expect the world to love their music as much as they do. Remember, an audience wants to be entertained. 'Make 'em laugh,' as Donald O'Connor sang in *Singin' in the Rain.*

"There's a big world out there with vast opportunities for people who play and love music," says Devine. "Very few people become international pop stars, but many, many individuals make a living in music—church organists/choir directors, piano teachers, studio engineers, songwriters, studio players, school music teachers, whatever! Find out what your whatever is!"

### Meet McNeil Johnston

McNeil Johnston grew up in Honolulu, Hawaii, and then attended Mannes College of Music in New York, majoring in music theory and music composition. Today he serves as a partner and the musical director of Outland Productions.

"I've been a musician all my life," says Johnston. "Piano since age four, violin since age ten, composing for orchestra by the sixth grade. There was never any question in my heart as to my overall career choice. I decided in college that composition suited me best. Aspiring to an instrumental performance career was too much pressure, too much work (and practice!), and a bit too limiting creatively.

"My job is one of constant variety. At any given moment, I may be orchestrating another composer's work, recording a jingle or two, writing my own music, or scoring a video. Typically I'm up at 6:30 A.M. I act as both Mr. Mom and Mr. Music as I try to work in my basement studio while seeing to my two daughters' needs and whims. Late at night (between 10:00 P.M. and 2:00 A.M.), I put in many additional hours while the family is asleep.

"I write a lot of commercially oriented music using MIDI technology because I've found that it's a very efficient and speedy way to 'write.' I play parts into the sequencer, edit on the computer, and, voila, music! Busy? Relaxed? Both!

"I love the fact that I get work in spurts, feast or famine. I thrive on tight deadlines and doing the impossible. I enjoy working at home using my own equipment for the most part, though I am occasionally found in larger recording studios. I work as much as is necessary, so the amount of hours per week varies between zero and one hundred!

"What I love about my work is that it's *my* work. As a composer/orchestrator, I put my stamp on everything I do. It's about as close to pure creativity as you can get and still get paid for doing it. What I don't like is that I'm occasionally wide open to criticism by the musically challenged. I've had a couple of what I call comebackers: orchestrations or compositions that were rejected for silly reasons that have very little to do with music.

"I'd advise other aspiring composers and songwriters to keep plugging, praying, preparing, practicing, and perspiring. Also, never never never even pretend you think you might know everything there is to know about what you do. Remember, there's a word for the moment we stop learning—DEATH!"

## FOR MORE INFORMATION

Academy of Country Music (ACM)
P.O. Box 508
Hollywood, CA 90078

American Composers Alliance
170 West Seventy-Fourth Street
New York, NY 10023

American Society of Composers and
Publishers (ASCAP)
1 Lincoln Plaza
New York, NY 10023

American Society of Music Copyists
(ASMC)
Box 2557
Times Square Station
New York, NY 10108

Composers Recording, Inc.
170 West Seventy-Fourth Street
New York, NY 10023

Meet the Composer, Inc.
2112 Broadway, Suite 505
New York, NY 10023

Nashville Songwriters Association
International (NSAI)
803 Eighteenth Street South
Nashville, TN 37203

National Association of Composers,
USA (NACUSA)
P.O. Box 49652
Barrington Station
Los Angeles, CA 90049

New Dramatists
424 West Forty-Fourth Street
New York, NY 10003

The Songwriters Guild
276 Fifth Avenue
New York, NY 10001